A GIRL'S GUIDE TO
decorating

abigail ahern

photography by Graham Atkins-Hughes

Quadrille
PUBLISHING

texture 120

creating texture • surface texture • flooring

light 144

light up your life • lighting effects • window treatments

practical stuff 174

tool kit essentials • tips and techniques

updating your home

Congratulations! You've got the pad – but it's a style disaster, a little more crash than flash. Before you panic, look beyond the sad décor and last-century fixtures and you could find that a few simple revamps would easily sort it out. By dipping your toe into DIY (in a very Sunday afternoon kind of way) you can effortlessly turn bland and boring into snazzy and super-cool. It's cheap, it's easy and it's highly addictive. What's exciting about interiors right now is that virtually anything goes. So, with a pinch of creativity, an eye for a bargain and a few tricks of the trade, you can turn a gloomy, outdated space into a complete Aladdin's cave of gorgeousness.

This traditional period home has received an up-to-the-minute, girl's guide makeover. Wooden floors, walls and doors have been given a lick of paint in a dense shade, providing the ideal backdrop for the fluorescent pink spray-painted occasional table. Team this up with an assortment of junk-shop lamps, interesting artwork and whimsical wallpaper and the room becomes a talking point. Shabby chic and industrial high tech should meet more often!

choosing your style

The hottest trend in decorating today is eclecticism. So whether you want a uniform scheme throughout your home or a medley of styles and periods, it's all about visual juxtaposition and an abundance of fun. But how do you achieve a look that not only surprises the eye, playing around with scale and colour, texture and light, but is at the same time harmonious and balanced? The key to success is to have something that seamlessly holds it all together – it could be a paint colour, textural feature or your choice of furnishings. A unifying element will leave you the freedom to fill your home with the things you love. Bedazzle away!

Artistic, personal, with a dash of quirkiness thrown in, this dressing area is anything but static. Here an unrestrained combination of feminine textures is the binding element, while a period figurative painting and vintage bottles create further layers in the look.

assessing your options

Before you embark on any project you should always think about your space and the role you want it to play. Stand back and take a good look: perhaps two small rooms would benefit from knocking through into one, or the fixtures in a bathroom need to be re-sited. Structural and demolition work, specialist skills such as plastering, carpentry and bricklaying, as well as anything involving plumbing, electricity and gas, are best left to those in the know and may well be beyond your budget. But if you can't afford a major revamp, don't despair. Homes will benefit just as much from a thorough overhaul of the décor. And there are tons of things you can do yourself without calling in the pros. The word DIY sounds scary but it really doesn't have to be.

Knocking through a wall to create an internal 'window' allows a visual flow between two rooms, but painting the rooms white is an easy way to give the impression of more space and light. The ledge itself becomes a place to show off personal effects, while the chalkboard, scribbled with the day's musings, injects an element of humour.

big ideas, small budget

As any girl knows, style has absolutely nothing to do with money, so limited funds needn't mean limited ideas. It's a uniquely personalized look that you want. Make a splash by transforming walls and floors with the intoxicating power of paint and pattern. Inject new life to tired furniture by giving it a rock-'n'-roll spray-paint makeover or fabulous new handles. Or wow your friends with an unusual display of artwork and photos. Customize, re-work and reinvent: your home will be given a modern jolt that turns it from faded to fabulous – and all without breaking the bank.

A few low-cost ideas have made this living room very chic. The basic, shop-bought shelf has been made chunkier and hung close to the floor for maximum impact. A sprayed-on coat of glossy black paint transforms the second-hand picture frame, while an intense, unified colour scheme for the walls and floor really sets off a glamorous feature light.

get creative

If I only ever gave one piece of advice to DIY novices it would be: go for it! Too often we get put off doing simple things, thinking they are jobs for professional decorators or those with specialist design knowledge. But you'll find loads of tips in this book to help you achieve your decorating dreams, whether it be for using effective colour schemes, deciding on the best window treatments, adding architectural features to your room – and not forgetting the all-important, glamorous touches that will make that space really yours.

Still thinking about whether to start that overhaul? I didn't think so!

Piles of books and magazines stashed in alcove shelves, on floors and around furniture like this desk bureau create an informal, makeshift library. Arranged beautifully in orderly stacks according to size and colour, they also provide great plinths for displaying treasured keepsakes.

TOM
FORD

JACQUES HELLEU & CHANEL

MODIGLIANI

JULIAN SCHNABEL

STYLIST

Gerhard
Richter

LOOS

Atlas

BOB RICHARDSON

Le Corbusier

MARIO TESTINO PORTRAITS

ELLIOTT ERWITT PERSONAL BEST

HAMPTONS

LEIBOVITZ A Photographer's Life 1990-2005

ANDREAS H. BITESNICH Polanude

BOMBAY

KENDRICK'S

BLACK LABEL

JEAN-MICHEL FRANK

TONY DUQ

noguchi

CLAUDE & FRANÇOIS-XAVIER LALA

Cy Pollacco   Cycles and Seasons

Libraries

Jacques Quinet

Castelli

The Houses of Philip Johnson

PIET MONDRIAN

Richard Meier

BRUEGEL

TOULOUSE-LAUTREC

PICASSO

GAUGUIN

TURNER

GOYA

REMBRANDT

INGRES

PISSARRO

MICHELANGELO

RAPHAEL

MODIGLIANI

planning

planning your space

Before rushing into any changes, stop for a moment to consider exactly what you will use your space for. It sounds obvious, doesn't it, but all good design should be planned around lifestyle, addressing three key elements: function, composition and style. So start with some questions: is this room somewhere you will entertain, sleep, eat or relax? Or perhaps it will be multi-functional, in which case it might be better to create different 'zones' for each activity. Analyse the good and bad points of the room: do you want to hide ugly features like radiators and highlight focal points like a fireplace or French windows? To help you create a structure that works, draw a floor plan to scale and experiment with layouts. Some basic tips: a U-shaped seating area is a lot more conducive to an intimate chat, while side tables or lamps arranged in pairs help with balance. And where possible, move furniture away from walls as this will make the space flow. Finally, what mood do you want to create – cosy, glamorous, formal? Let the fun begin…

Smaller rooms with many functions, like this living room with a working area, are more difficult to divide into zones, so think instead about unifying the junctions between areas. Using furniture that isn't typically 'home office' allows this workspace to blend with the rest of the room. Colour-coordinated files and stylish storage boxes keep stressful clutter at bay and are used in tones that complement the overall décor.

planning your space
multi-use rooms

Few of us have the luxury of a room for each function of the home – modern-day spaces have to work much harder. Zoning off sounds a little severe but it's the best way of making multi-use rooms feel more intimate and of concealing areas you don't want on view. If you need to create a home office area or a quiet nook for reading, for example, a decorative screen, a free-standing bookcase (page 42) or even a group of large plants can provide a simple partition. These devices will stop the space feeling cavernous in larger, single-purpose rooms, too. If a physical barrier would be too obtrusive in a smaller room, lay different rugs in separate zones to give each area its own personality. Whatever you choose, dividing your space according to function creates essential pockets of privacy, leaving you free to work, read and relax.

The floor-to-ceiling windows are the focal point of this living room and the furniture arrangement complements this. The sofas and chairs are positioned for conversation, and the shapes are kept simple, with the large rug helping to separate the seating area from the rest of the room.

TOP TIP: Use textured rugs and pouffes to soften the geometric lines of a room.

planning your space
small and light

Small spaces demand ingenuity: it's much harder to make them look good. You may not be able to change the physical dimension of your room but you can do a huge amount to influence the perception of its size. Keep furniture to a minimum and get creative with your storage (page 41) and the space will immediately feel larger. Dress windows simply to allow as much natural light in as possible. A pale colour scheme can help turn bijou spaces into light, airy rooms. Passive and neutral colours make walls and furniture recede, opening out the space and making it appear bigger than it really is. The key to preventing it from being bland is to add visual interest through pattern and texture, in the wallpaper and furnishings, for example. This will infuse your space with life and define its personality.

A neutral palette maximizes the space in this tiny bedroom. There is a subtle pattern to the wallpaper, but otherwise walls are left bare and furnishings are kept to a minimum, creating an oasis of calm. The same colour scheme has been applied to adjoining rooms so that the door can remain open, allowing the eye to flow between them – another illusion of space.

see also:
colour p88
light p151

planning your space
small and dark

Spatially challenged dark rooms are my idea of heaven: cosy, intimate, dramatic, snug – the list is endless. And it's a big fat myth that a dark colour scheme automatically makes a room look smaller. What tiny spaces can't deal with is a jarring array of shades, so keep contrasts to a minimum. Using the same shade on the walls, floor and ceiling makes the lines between them blur, disguising the limited area. A good lighting scheme is a transforming element for a small, dark space. Recessed halogens in the ceiling, positioned around the perimeter of the room, can fool the eye by appearing to push back the walls. Another trick of the trade is to paint the ceiling with a high-glamour coat of epoxy paint, giving it the glossy finish of lacquer to make the light bounce off. A small room can't change its size – it's all about working with what you've got.

Inviting, sumptuous and super-sexy, deepest black on the walls and ceiling of this bedroom give it high drama. Strategically placed table lamps draw the eye into the corners of the room and soften the moody palette with pools of light.

see also:
colour p92
light p157

TOP TIP: Don't move: improve! Paint easily transforms featureless rooms into super-exciting spaces.

room analysis

Knocking through between the kitchen and dining room is a major job, but even simple changes can make a big impact.

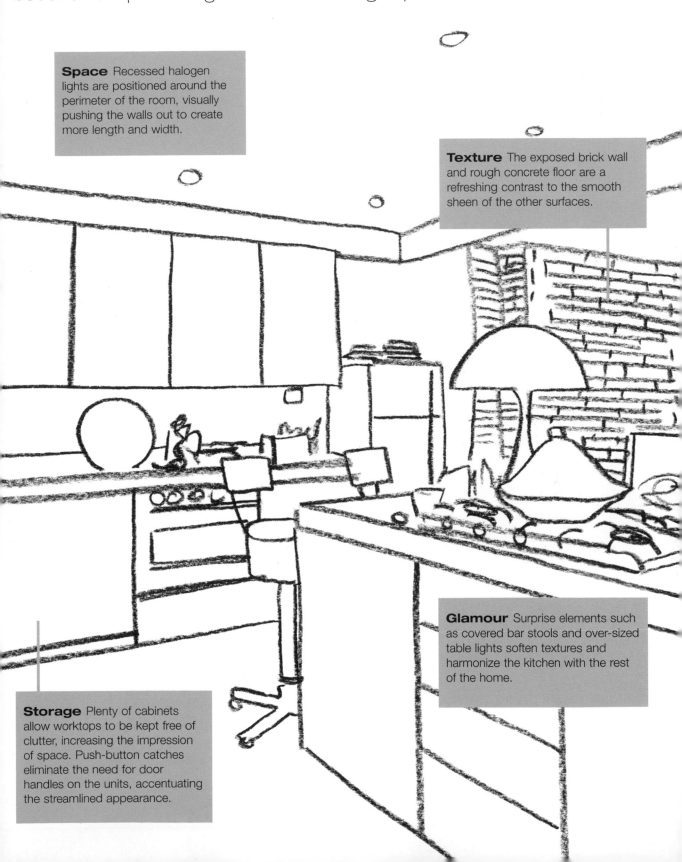

Space Recessed halogen lights are positioned around the perimeter of the room, visually pushing the walls out to create more length and width.

Texture The exposed brick wall and rough concrete floor are a refreshing contrast to the smooth sheen of the other surfaces.

Glamour Surprise elements such as covered bar stools and over-sized table lights soften textures and harmonize the kitchen with the rest of the home.

Storage Plenty of cabinets allow worktops to be kept free of clutter, increasing the impression of space. Push-button catches eliminate the need for door handles on the units, accentuating the streamlined appearance.

planning your space
kitchens

We all covet a kitchen that not only looks beautiful but also makes the best use of the space. Start by assessing your kitchen according to each function – prepping, cooking, washing, storage and so on – and plan how much room each task needs and how one will flow into another. Decide which part you want to commit to seating and incorporate that into your design. (A large table won't fit in a small kitchen but a little breakfast perch just might.) And if you can't change the layout itself then there are many innovative storage solutions to help you maximize your space. It takes a little research – but it will make spending time in your kitchen an absolute pleasure.

Stacks of recipe books and other collectables have been skilfully arranged on open shelving, turning a traditional kitchen storage area into a stylish focal point.

Space-saving doesn't have to be dull. Eye-level shelves house simple groupings of plates, glasses and other odds and ends, creating visual interest but keeping worktop clutter at bay. Tear sheets from magazines become a temporary art installation and give an otherwise practical space a bit of an edge.

see also:
glamour p65

planning your space
bathrooms

Planning your bathroom can feel like doing a jigsaw puzzle: there are a number of set elements (basin, toilet and so on) that you must somehow fit together. Replacing everything can be expensive, but keeping new fixtures in the same position will help cut costs on labour. Make sure you have plenty of storage – you can almost never have enough for all your bits and bobs. A good overall lighting scheme is often neglected in bathrooms, as the typical focus is on task lighting – but if it's too bright it will feel institutional. So your scheme needs to be as flexible as possible: focused enough for applying make-up or shaving, but able to be dimmed when taking a deep, relaxing bath. Maximize natural daylight, add dimmers and consider putting the lights on different switches so that you can alter the mood.

A small bathroom feels airy when the space and décor are kept simple. Here, an unfussy roller blind lets natural light flood in and allows space for a small occasional table underneath the window. Quirky hand-shaped hooks for hanging towels and robes take clever advantage of the vertical wall space.

see also:
glamour p59
light p146

the illusion of space
long and narrow

There is no getting away from the fact that long, narrow rooms present challenges. It is difficult to arrange furniture successfully and the space can easily look unbalanced. Long rooms need be broken up visually, so consider placing furniture diagonally rather than against the wall. Trick the eye by painting the longest wall in a light colour to recede. An arrangement of shelves or a quirky display of art makes the shorter walls in the room appear wider, as does using wallpaper with a bold pattern or scale. Avoiding casting too much light on the ceiling as this will emphasize its shape; ambient and mood lighting should come to the fore. Armed with these techniques, you can easily create different perspectives to disguise the nature of the room.

Yes, it's narrow, but that doesn't mean it has to look and feel like a corridor. Furniture in this home office is on a small scale but has been moved away from the walls to improve the visual flow, while the bold rug also attracts the eye. The window has been simply adorned with a lace curtain that draws little attention to the end of the room.

see also:
glamour p76
colour p88

the illusion of space
tricks with mirrors

Beautiful in themselves, mirrors are a super-stylish way to breathe new life into walls, but they can also brighten and expand your room with their transforming perspectives on light and space. Place a mirror (page 36) by a window, lamp or candle and the amount of light is instantly multiplied. When several mirrors are angled towards each other, so that the image is broken up, you have an ever-changing piece of artwork. Mirror choice is vast but a few simple pointers will help you figure out which to put where, and a combination of types always makes a striking installation. The important thing is to achieve both contrast and balance – with a bit of oomph thrown in. No wonder mirrors have become the designer's best friend!

Attention-grabbing mirrors such as these transform a plain wall into a highly original one – but they also make the hallway seem wider. Painting the frame the same colour as the walls helps increase the impression of space, and reflecting architectural elements such as the staircase is a simple, eye-catching trick.

Plain, flat mirrors are the most commonly used. The image reflected back is always the same size as the object, so they are perfect for bedrooms, bathrooms and working areas, where close examination is needed. When used without a frame, the great advantage is that they can be cut to any shape and size, enabling you to create your own designs.

Ultra-clear mirrors are similar to plain mirrors but are produced with a reduced iron content so that the glass loses its greenish tinge. The resulting reflection has improved clarity and is a truer representation of colour.

Bevelled mirrors have angled edges and are often frameless. The edge acts as a prism, creating colourful, intense reflections of light, which in turn add depth and character to the mirror. Great in living and dining rooms, they add vibrancy to your scheme.

Concave mirrors, where the glass is curved inwards, are good in dressing rooms and bathrooms as they enlarge reflections, enhance space and focus light towards one point.

Convex mirrors have the opposite effect as the glass curves outwards, creating condensed reflections. They can make large rooms feel cosier and more intimate.

Feature mirrors and frames, such as antique (genuine or reproduction) or tinted ones, add pizzazz to any room. Frame choice opens up another vista of design. Elaborately carved or simply crafted, cowhide or mother of pearl, the key is to make sure it complements the overall scheme. So a room filled with bold, statement furniture can take a mirror with a heavy, ornate frame.

how to...
hang a mirror

Heavy objects like mirrors require a more robust way of hanging than simply banging in a nail. Wallplugs, which secure themselves to the wall cavity and prevent the screws falling out, are the key to a simple and safe way to display.

shopping list

mirror of choice
stud finder (optional)
carpenter's pencil
variable-speed drill
   plus bits
wallplug
hammer
screw
screwdriver

TOP TIP: Wrap a little piece of tape around the drill bit at the same depth as your wallplug so you know exactly how deep to drill.

1 First things first: ascertain what type of wall you have (concrete, plaster, brick, partition). Fixings in plaster and partition walls need the additional support of the internal wooden studs for heavy items such as mirrors. You can tap the wall to find where it is most solid or use a stud finder (page 181). This will also help you avoid pipes and electricity cables.

2 Select an appropriately sized screw and wallplug for the job (follow the manufacturer's guidelines). Mark a suitable place away from pipes and cables, and over an upright stud if necessary. Remember that the supporting wire or chain may cause the mirror to hang lower than you expect.

3 Drill a hole in the wall (page 181) the depth of the wallplug with a drill bit that is slightly larger than the screw. (If unsure, start off with one that seems a little too small and re-drill with a larger bit afterwards.) Concrete and brick walls require a special masonry drill bit and a drill with a masonry action known as 'hammering'. Try to keep the drill bit at right angles to the wall and drill in a single action with even pressure.

4 Clear off any debris and insert the wallplug all the way into the hole, tapping it in lightly with a hammer if necessary. Fix the screw into the wallplug (page 181), leaving approximately 10mm proud of the wall. Carefully hook the string or chain on the back of the mirror over the screw and adjust so that it hangs squarely. Make sure it is properly secure and stand back to admire!

creating more space

Space is what we crave most in our homes, so obsessive hoarders listen up: too much clutter decreases space, both physically and visually, so be ruthless! You don't have to banish everything – open shelves are wonderful for adding tons more storage and at the same time showing your taste to the world. Select furniture that is in keeping with the size of the room: low-slung ottomans, coffee tables or chairs without arms are less imposing. In kitchens and bathrooms fit cabinets with push-to-open latches as these will add to the feeling of spaciousness. Use a cool palette in your decorating scheme, as it will open out your room, and any room will appear larger if it's well lit by a combination of natural and artificial light.

Space around a sink is used to maximum effect. Functional objects have been displayed with great panache by grouping and clustering according to a neutral palette. The strategically placed artwork prevents the room from becoming too 'kitchen-like'.

see also:
glamour p60; p65
colour p96

creating more space
small rooms

Chucking out what you don't need will work wonders, but if you seriously can't part with stuff then at least invest in some multi-purpose furniture – beds with drawers underneath, stools with lifting lids. Fill empty fireplaces with books and magazines, and wall-mount TV and music equipment to increase floor space. Wardrobes are not just for your Jimmy Choos: tuck DVDs, books, blankets, anything that is not in continual use, behind closed doors. Move furniture away from walkways to open up the space. Get creative with colour and lighting and your space won't feel nearly as cramped. The eye zips round small rooms in next to no time, so everything needs to have impact and style.

The lines between the bold wallpaper and the painted black cabinets and door merge seamlessly in this minuscule kitchen, where every inch of storage space has been used, even above the cupboards. Concealed under-cupboard lighting is another space-saver.

see also:
colour p110
light p154

creating more space
shelving

Whether tucked in alcoves or hung on a feature wall, shelving is vital for maximizing space. Shelves are fab for stashing books, personal mementos and all sorts of bits and pieces, and untidy ones can be easily concealed behind curtains. But many shelves are works of art in their own right and so the difficulty will be choosing between the seemingly endless types. Do you want fixed and formulaic units or freestanding and casual ones? An industrial metal vibe or something more homely like wood? It's good to use a liberal mix of styles – it allows for more creativity and the result won't appear too homogenized. Just remember to artfully hide your stuff away or display it with flair.

Free-standing shelving is informal in look and allows for the greatest flexibility, as you can move the unit around to suit. Typically placed against a wall, it can also be used to divide spaces (page 20). Flat-pack units are usually easy to install (page 48) and any free-standing unit can be taken with you when you move.

Fixed bracket shelves are the most straightforward type (page 44), with brackets or battens fixed to the wall and the shelving simply placed across or screwed to them. Brackets can be exposed or concealed, depending on the design. The shelves come in different materials and finishes, you can choose between various widths and depths, plus they are relatively easy to remove if you need to. For greater visual impact you can box out a basic shelf to make it chunkier.

Built-in shelves make great use of alcove space. Supported by brackets or battens as for fixed bracket shelves, they can also be boxed out for effect. The alcove itself becomes the shelf's two vertical ends, providing useful support for books, and painting the shelves the same colour as the walls helps them to recede, enhancing the impression of space.

Adjustable shelving systems use vertical side rails with movable brackets, enabling you to adjust the spacing between the shelves. This is handy when displaying or storing a variety of different-sized objects, but they can look a touch basic unless they have been custom made.

Suspended shelves, where the surface is suspended from wires in the wall or ceiling, are more aesthetic than practical, as each shelf can only hold loads of up to 8kg. Typically made from glass, they can give a floaty, ethereal look to your display.

Style and content really complement each other in this storage system: piles of hefty books look their best on robust, boxed-out shelves. Painted the same colour as the walls, the horizontal lines of the built-in shelving help the alcove seem wider.

see also:
glamour p66; p68

how to...

put up shelves

Perfect for that ever-rotating display of curiosities, shelves are there to get creative with. And with a stylish range of pre-cut kits at your fingertips, putting them up couldn't be easier.

shopping list

shelf and bracket kit
stud finder (optional)
retractable tape measure
spirit level
carpenter's pencil
variable-speed drill plus bits
wallplugs
screws
screwdriver

1 First you need to figure out the type of wall you have (concrete, plaster, brick, partition). Solid walls need a more powerful drill to make the holes (page 176) but can take heavier weights. If your walls are partition, you will need to locate the upright wooden studs either by tapping to find where it is most solid or by using a stud finder (page 181) and then fasten the brackets to these for extra support.

2 Taking into account the position of pipes, cables and studs, decide on the position of the shelf or shelves on the wall – you may want them evenly spaced or irregular for a quirkier look. Starting with the highest shelf, hold the bracket up to the wall with a spirit level on top and mark the position of the holes with a pencil.

3 Drill the hole for each of the screws, insert the wallplugs and screw the bracket to the wall (page 181). Most shelving requires a screw of at least 50mm and up to 75mm in length. For heavy loads you will need a thick screw gauge of around 10; for normal loads 6 or 7 is adequate.

4 Slide the shelf over the bracket and screw in. Screws are normally fixed underneath, but if your shelf is above eye level you may want to place the shelf upside down on the bracket so that the screws will not be visible. Repeat as necessary for further shelves.

TOP TIP: Using the longest and thickest screws possible will make the shelf sturdier and give you the flexibility to put heavier items on them in the future.

creating more space
cabinets

The world's your oyster when it comes to choosing storage cabinets: floor or wall mounted, free-standing or recessed (or maybe a combination of these). It sounds a little overwhelming but not if you decide in advance how they are going to fit in your room. Wall-mounted cabinets free up valuable floor space, but lower, freestanding ones provide not only hide-away storage but also a surface for display. Recessed cabinets are super-practical as they use the space within the wall's void, saving valuable inches while giving you a bespoke fixture. So whether ready-made or custom-made, cabinets all do the same job – it just comes down to budget and personal preference.

Flat-pack cabinets are cheap, stylish, easy to assemble (page 48) and readily available. Yes, you can buy them straight off the shelves, jump in a cab and take them home with you immediately – heaven. They are manufactured in a limited number of widths and design options so you won't get that 'one of a kind' look, although there are possibilities for customizing by spray painting or adding different handles, for example.

Ready-made cabinets can be bought from many high-street furniture outlets, with no assembly required. The only challenge is to get them home – so don't forget to factor in the cost of van hire or a delivery charge. Choices of material are greater than for flat-packs but are still relatively limited. However, by selecting stock cabinets you can upgrade to a more luxurious finish when your budget allows.

Semi-custom-made cabinets are also factory made but your choices increase. You can dictate the size, which is useful if your room is too small to accommodate ready-made furniture, and you get many more options on material and finish.

Custom-made cabinets are the most expensive and have the longest lead time (the time before you receive the finished product). Crafted especially for you, every element can be tailored to your needs. Awkward corners, unsightly electrical appliances and mundane kitchen equipment can all be concealed by bespoke cabinets – at a cost – and the result will be spectacular.

Feature furniture, that one-off, eye-catching centrepiece, will certainly give you a tingle, but be careful you don't compromise on the storage it affords. It is unlikely to be a bargain, so you have to be sure it will earn its keep.

This wall-mounted cabinet, hung along one wall, not only appears to lengthen the room but also brings it to life with its eclectic display. Painted the same colour as the walls, the cabinet blends into the décor, while push-to-open latches (page 60) maintain a streamlined, contemporary look.

see also:
glamour p84
light p160

*how to...

make up a flat-pack cabinet

Self-assembly furniture strikes fear into even the most experienced DIY-ers. But take heart: some simple steps will ensure the task goes smoothly – and by thinking outside the box you can make it a really special feature of your room.

shopping list
(will vary according to item)

flat-pack cabinet of choice
screwdriver (cross- or flat-head)
variable-speed drill plus bits
adhesive gun
g-clamp
hammer
carpenter's pencil
wallplugs
screws
screwdriver

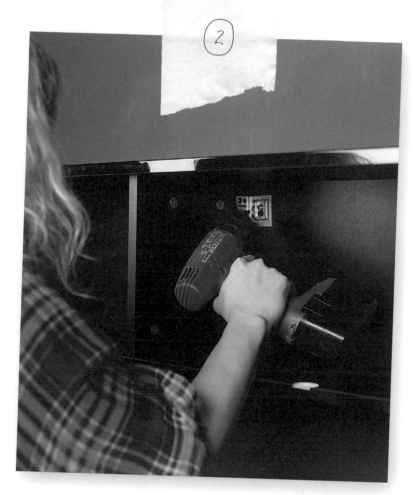

1 First read the instructions carefully and check out the illustrations, as things often go wrong when the assembly order is not strictly followed. Make sure you have plenty of time and all the tools to hand before you start – you don't want to interrupt the task with an emergency dash to the DIY store.

2 Clear a table and set out all the panels, screws and fittings that came with your flat-pack. Tick off each piece against the contents list. Flat-packs often use dowels (little wooden pins tapped into holes and held together with wood adhesive), so check you have the correct number. If pieces are missing then back to the store it goes.

3 Follow the step-by-step instructions on the pack – you can cross off the steps as you go if it helps – but don't be tempted to take short cuts or invent your own method if the pieces do not fit together immediately. Better to take a quick break and come back to it, or call a friend or a helpline (if there is one): two heads are better than one.

4 Once your cabinet is complete, why not hang it on a wall for an unusual, space-saving effect? Drill four holes through the back of the cabinet wide enough to take a size 10 screw. Prop the cabinet against the wall and mark the position of the holes with a pencil. (You may need to use a stud finder to check for pipes and electricity cables, or to locate wall studs for extra support – see page 181.) Place the cabinet back down, drill the wall holes and insert wallplugs. Finally, hoist the cabinet back into position – with help, if necessary – and screw into place (page 181).

5 Finally, a bit of good news for the future: scientists are working on 'smart' flat-packs (fitted with microchips that flash to show which piece fits where). Music to our ears!

TOP TIP: A tray with separate compartments stops screws, nails and dowels rolling away and allows for easy access during the job.

glamour

✳ the wow factor

Turning your space into a fabulously stylish pad is what interior decorating is all about. But how to achieve that elusive wow factor? You don't have to have an A-list budget or even a personal stylist to live a life of glitz and glamour – there are simpler ways and means. Glam homes banish clutter behind closed doors, opening up the space and allowing the eye to take in a stunning piece of statement furniture, say, or an invigorating colour scheme. Good lighting is vital for any room to look its best, while playing around with textures and patterns, styles and scale contributes to that all-important X factor. But perhaps the most important element is to really make the space yours. Mix and match styles of furniture and décor in your own unique way and they'll become a talking point. Display your quirky knick-knacks with chutzpah and you'll create a home that's like no other.

Sometimes less is more. This stylish wall light enlivens an otherwise simply decorated wall, and its glass petals reflect and bounce the light beautifully around the space. The vintage bedside table is a one-off find, its understated form adding calm elegance.

see also:
planning p38
light p146

the wow factor
ditching convention

Why follow the crowd? Adding a touch of unconventionality here and a dash of eccentricity there is the magic that binds a space together. You shouldn't ditch the rule book entirely, but a tongue-in-cheek approach to old traditions won't go amiss. Even putting familiar items in an unfamiliar setting can create a startling effect. So be unpredictable: juxtapose, say, a worn leather chair, a fabulously ornate mirror and a down-to-earth sisal rug. Place that hammered tin bowl you picked up in India centre-stage on a low-slung glass coffee table. Line the walls in your loo with over-the-top fancy wallpaper. You get the idea.

This bathroom has movie star written all over it. Vintage finds from a range of eras, an abundance of gloss and shine, combined with wallpaper to die for, all work to create an opulent room that delights the eye. Who would have expected to find such star quality in this tiny space?

Glamorous touches in your home are the trend of the moment and create a truly electrifying effect.

Colour Set against a deep, sumptuous background, bright colours will really pop out at you. Keeping furniture within the same tonal range looks very sleek and helps a bulky item recede.

Lighting Mix and match pendant, table and floor lights in a variety of styles for a highly personalized, layered look.

Style Cushions are easy to place so go all-out bold. An animal-inspired lamp adds a touch of fun to the scheme, while unusual artwork and panels of fabric on the walls keep things interesting.

Texture The staple of every girl's handbag, gloss reflects the light beautifully and adds a touch of instant glamour.

{ **TOP TIP:** Painting cupboards in a colour with a similar depth of tone to the walls helps them to blend in seamlessly. }

the wow factor

easy-to-change features

I've said it before and I'll say it again: adding glamour doesn't have to cost big bucks. Reinvent and embellish existing pieces and you'll create a bespoke, sophisticated and individual look much more cheaply and easily. Kitchens and bathrooms often present the most problems because they are expensive to change completely. So think instead of updating kitchen cabinets by elongating the length of the doors (page 60) and painting them in an eye-popping shade. Bravo! Want trendy hotel luxury in your bathroom? Then ditch that old bath tap for an over-sized, spa-type model. Replace standard wardrobe door handles with funky ones (page 84) or box out a standard shelf (page 68). It's those easy-to-add details that make all the difference. Now the real trick is to mix it all up: a huge mirror with a little table underneath, the odd super-sized piece of furniture in a tiny room. It's exciting, frolicsome and unapologetically uplifting!

Very much the centre of the home, the kitchen deserves special attention. We want it stylishly cool, yet ordered and functional. Elongating cupboard doors does just this and is a simple, inexpensive trick that looks indulgent and luxurious.

see also:
planning p28; p30
colour p94

how to...

make over-sized cupboard doors

Over-sized cupboard doors look especially modern and streamlined without handles. When fitted with 180-degree hinges they fold almost flat to the wall – ideal for maximum access.

shopping list

retractable tape measure
MDF
eggshell or gloss paint
paint brush
180-degree hinges
carpenter's pencil
variable-speed drill
  plus bits
screwdriver
screws
push-to-open latches

1 Measure the size of the cupboard externally and calculate the width of the doors, less 3mm to allow them to open. Decide on the length of the new doors, remembering to leave at least a 30mm gap from the floor for cleaning. Have your MDF cut to size at a DIY store and paint both sides with your chosen shade. Allow to dry.

2 Lay the doors down on the floor and place the hinges at one edge, equally spaced from the top and bottom, but not wider apart than the height of the cabinet. Mark the position with a pencil and, placing an off-cut of wood underneath, drill the holes and screw the hinges into the door (page 181).

3 Now hold the door at 90 degrees to the cabinet. Mark the holes for the screws on the cabinet and drill – it is likely the new site will be closer to the top and bottom of the cabinet than the original hinge so as to properly support the larger doors. Screw the hinges firmly into the cabinet.

4 Finally, screw the push-to-open latch into the cabinet at the top corner. A light touch of the finger and – voila! – your super-glam door springs open.

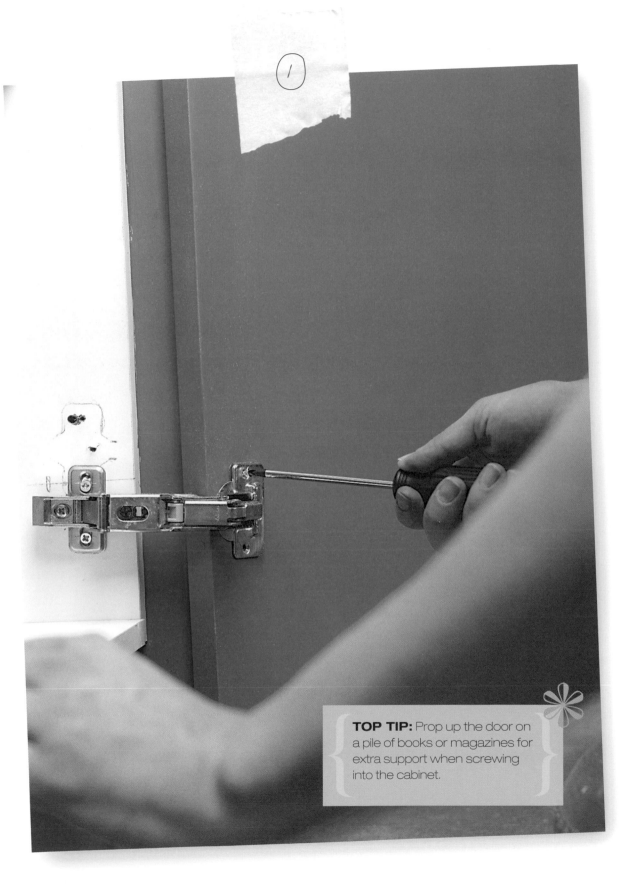

TOP TIP: Prop up the door on a pile of books or magazines for extra support when screwing into the cabinet.

displaying trophies

Displaying personal treasures, such as photographs, books, jewellery and mementos from far-flung places, gives a home a heart and soul. So instead of storing them away in the attic, ensure that such curiosities get the kudos they deserve. All too often, however, shelves and mantelpieces, coffee tables and bookcases become an unsightly muddle, so you'll need a few design tips (page 66) to make the most of your display. One foolproof way is to group according to colour – a heap of the latest reads, laid to reveal their colourful spines, becomes a wonderful plinth for a hand-thrown ceramic bowl, for example. Or cluster by texture: scraps of roughly hewn wood alongside wooden artefacts and over-sized bead necklaces. Odd numbers work better visually than even, as does varying the height of the objects or zig-zagging items instead of just putting them in a straight line. Arrange your trophies in this way and you'll have no trouble making beautiful still-life displays.

Artwork and objects are united by a limited palette of neutrals, with the odd punch of colour thrown in. Whether standing alone or clustered in groups, each item is surrounded by space to help the visual flow.

see also:
intro p14
colour p91

displaying trophies
kitchen displays

We often fall into the trap of thinking a kitchen is just about functionality, yet as the social hub of the home, it can be the area in which we spend the most time. So why waste an opportunity to create masterpieces of display that really reflect you? Clearing worktops of unnecessary mess and rarely used kitchen gadgets is the first creative step to make. Now you have room to devote a section to an impromptu minibar, another nook for a display of favourite recipe books. Heap brightly coloured tea towels in groups and fill bowls with lemons or limes for an added splash of colour. Cluster tea lights on surfaces for an unexpected, after-dark effect. Even those essential functional items like kettles and toasters can add great visual interest and texture – they just need to be displayed with aplomb.

Placing an unexpected piece of furniture such as this vintage glazed cabinet in the kitchen takes the room from utilitarian to glamorous. It sets a specific tone so that even something as ordinary as a selection of glassware can be imaginatively displayed, making it an equal part of the design.

displaying trophies
shelf displays

Shelf displays only work when objects – no matter how grand or trivial – are arranged in aesthetically pleasing rhythms. It's not about being cowed by a rigid scheme, but unless the juxtaposition of each object is right, your design will feel disjointed and out of kilter. How the eye flows from one object to the next will be determined by the shape and size of each item. In addition, every shelf has to have 'negative' space, which allows groupings or stand-alone pieces to breathe. These factors also dictate the mood, so a serene shelving display will be one where all objects are similar in size and equally placed; larger objects with unusual shapes or bold hues set a more energetic tone. By all means mix up your arrangements by perching, say, the odd globe next to pottery, books, pebbles and jewellery – but just remember to balance the assortment with oodles of space and the occasional bit of symmetry.

Symmetry is the matching element in a design scheme and can be achieved in a variety of ways. Think twin lamps or a collection of photo frames in similar sizes and styles. Objects can either be arranged outwards from the central point of the shelf or balanced equally working in from its ends. Symmetry makes for a harmonious, calming effect but, used excessively, can sometimes lead to dull and lifeless displays.

Asymmetry, where the difference between objects is deliberately embraced, is a harder feature to get right. Consider, for example, a large vase containing a floral arrangement at one end and a grouping of candelabras at the other. The overall shape of both is similar, but the scale and weight of them are not, thereby creating a real sense of playfulness. Too much asymmetry

see also:
colour p96

creates an uncomfortable jumble, however, so use in moderation.

Themed groups, such as those united by texture, colour or even a particular style or era, can help to avoid rampant eclecticism. Again, it's not something you need to go overboard with – you don't want to seem like a control freak – but any one of these elements can draw together objects in a pleasing and stimulating way.

Mixing it up is the key to a vibrant yet balanced display – the reality is that professionals draw on all of the above techniques when creating their designs. So play around with the forms and scale, as well as the colours and textures of the objects on your shelves. It's not adhering to any one style but the mix that makes it interesting.

Shelves that float on the wall hold an arty selection of objects, arranged according to scale and colour. The items are broken up with bursts of negative space, which helps to emphasize each group.

TOP TIP: Using a toning palette of cool colours enhances the feeling of space in smaller rooms.

how to...

box out shelves

Fattening up a standard skinny shelf into a chunkier, funkier model is as cheap as chips – but the result will look far more expensive.

shopping list

shelf and bracket kit
MDF
retractable tape measure
wood adhesive
adhesive gun (optional)
caulk
sandpaper
paint
paint brush

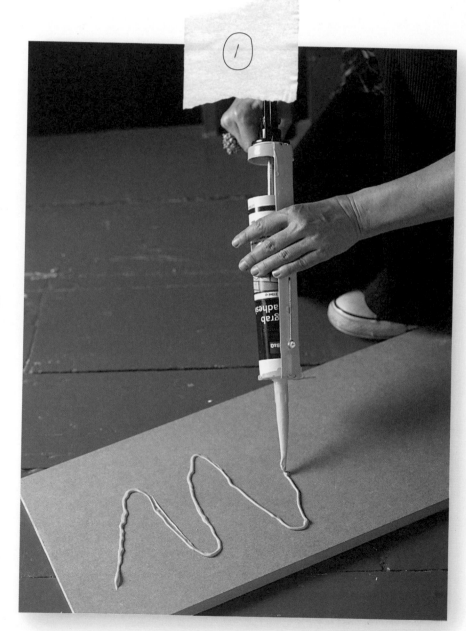

2

TOP TIP: Using an adhesive gun makes the flow of adhesive far easier to control.

1 Put up the standard shelf in the method described earlier (page 44). To make a boxy shelf you need to create three new fascias: for the top, front and underside. The front fascia will be the same width and height as the original shelf. To calculate the size of the top and underside, measure the depth of the existing shelf and add the thickness of the MDF to your measurement (the width will be the same as for the original shelf). Have your lengths cut to size at a DIY store.

2 Apply the adhesive to the back of the boards in a zig-zag fashion and press each piece firmly to the existing shelf. Leave to dry for the amount of time recommended by the manufacturer.

3 When the new fascias are fully bonded, caulk the gaps (page 183) and sand off any excess for a smooth finish.

4 Paint as desired for a truly sensational look, remembering to clean the brush thoroughly afterwards (page 180).

personal details

Filling your pad with stuff that makes you happy, whether it be personal photographs, coveted books, that raffia basket you bought on holiday or a favourite toy from childhood, makes a unique, personalized space. You don't need to follow trends: create your own by looking at the place as your very own blank canvas. Bring it alive with objects that lift your spirits and conjure up wonderful memories. You can spend top whack on sofas, cabinets and up-to-the-minute entertainment systems, but they won't give you half as much satisfaction as the objects that are meaningful to you and you alone. When all the diverse elements of your past and present are brought together they tell a story: about you, the lifestyle you lead and the space you call home.

This regular household refrigerator quickly becomes a bespoke surface for keepsakes such as photographs, notes, postcards and trophy ribbons. Displaying in this way helps to create the personal narrative of a life.

personal details
photo displays

Personal photos – of friends, family, a funny event or an image of your childhood – provide no better story of you. Really special or intimate scenes are more appropriately placed in the bedroom or study, but more general framed pictures, or even a selection of loose prints on a mantelpiece in the living and dining rooms, can be a welcome introduction to visitors. But avoid hanging them in humid areas like the kitchen and bathroom, where even framed photos could be damaged.

Unframed photos neatly stuck to the wall give this highly personal album the status of a gallery wall. Other memories are evoked by a collection of items on the mantelpiece, each carrying its own visual weight.

Hanging artwork – whether an original canvas, a print reproduction or a photographic image – can make a huge impact in your home. But figuring out what you can live with long-term isn't always easy. Over time a very bold abstract might tire or clash with a change in décor, so take your time visiting art fairs, markets, galleries and auction houses – and don't buy unless you really can't leave without it. Original artwork needn't cost the earth: junk shops are good for bargain finds and look out for 'open house' events in artists' communities, where you can buy direct without paying a gallery commission.

Even a length of fancy wallpaper becomes a piece of art when casually hung from bulldog clips. Inexpensive and easy to change, it is an ever-evolving, casual way to display.

Mixing and matching picture styles and frames, as well as interspersing them with other objects like the giant lettering, reinforces the fun, eclectic mood of this home.

artwork
arranging pictures

How you arrange pictures can have as much impact as the artworks themselves. While some statement pieces deserve to be hung alone, others (such as drawings, photos and small-scale prints) work best in groups, clustered by a staircase, above a sofa or simply strung along a wall. Professional-looking hanging relies on a few simple principles. The important thing to remember is that the images together should create a visual rhythm that is greater than if each one were hung separately. When placing art around furniture go with your intuition: lowering an image to waist height relates it to, say, the sofa. But if you want to draw the eye upwards to highlight an architectural detail perhaps, then hang your picture higher to help accent it.

Grid formations are very balanced and work best with frames of identical size and style. Such simple symmetry also works well for unframed photographs (page 73), but can become a touch regimented if unrelieved by contrasting objects close by. You'll need to measure carefully (page 78) to ensure that the spaces between each picture are identical – any small variation or inaccuracy will immediately ruin the effect.

Horizontal or vertical lines of pictures, hung with ample breathing space in between, create a very modern look. They are fab for transitional areas such as hallways and stairwells, as they have the effect of leading the eye along the space – just don't squash them too tightly together. As with grid formations, accurate measurements are essential to the success of the scheme.

Organic clusters, varying in style and scale, resonate with boho chic, but can take a little time to work out. To avoid lopsidedness and unsightly clashes, think of your collection as a single image, grouping together subject matter, colours and frames and reducing the spaces between them to create seamless unity. Before you start banging in nails, cut paper to the size of each image and then temporarily fix to the wall, or lay all the pictures out on the floor, so that you can experiment with the design. It sounds like a hassle but this preparation will really improve the end result.

An organic cluster of images animates this bedroom wall. Some pictures lean against the wall for a relaxed feel, and the uneven spacing between them is also part of the composition, which has the impact of a large, single work without the formality.

see also:
light p157

TOP TIP: Wall-mounted lamps such as picture lights are a vital space-saver in small rooms.

TANIA

how to...

hang pictures with nails

Displaying artwork is a striking way of making a personal statement in your home. With this simple technique you can be sure that the arrangement will have maximum impact.

shopping list

artwork of choice
carpenter's pencil
retractable tape measure
hammer
nail(s)
spirit level
rubber

1 Heavy items on plaster or partition walls need to be hung using wallplugs (page 181) but for most pictures a simple nail will suffice. Decide where you would like your picture to hang and make a light pencil mark on the wall at each top corner. Measure and mark the centre point between the two.

2 Lay the picture face down on some soft fabric or carpet to prevent it from scratching. Measure and mark the centre point of the picture on the top of the frame.

3 To work out the height for the nail, pull the hanging wire taut towards the centre mark and measure from here to the top of the frame. Now transfer this measurement to the wall by measuring down the required distance from the centre point you made earlier.

4 Very wide or heavy pictures need to be hung from two points for extra support. Measure the same distance from each side of the frame and, pulling the wire taut, the distance between one of these points and the top of the frame. (Remember that the further apart these two points are the closer the picture will be to the wall.) Transfer the measurements to the wall in the same manner as described earlier.

5 Hammer the nail in at the lower mark at an upward angle so that the wall will take the weight rather than your nail, taking care not to bash your fingers (page 181). Leave approximately 10mm proud. Hang your picture and, using a spirit level, adjust until straight. Rub off any visible pencil marks.

TOP TIP: If your picture is quite large use a two-pin picture hook at each side: it will make it easier to hang straight and provide extra stability.

final details

Accessories are so easy to replace that you can afford to have a bit of fun with them. So whether it's with quick-to-arrange cushions, new bedding and rugs, or a speedy update of the door handles (page 84), follow in the footsteps of the fashion-forward and introduce over-sized elements in your design. It won't necessarily work in all situations – it's very much about experimenting. But your home will have heightened drama and become more exciting as a result.

Replacement fabric knobs on a chest of drawers work well with wood textures and bring a touch of the hand-crafted to the scheme.

Clever little revamps like replacing knobs and handles bring your doors and drawers bang up to trend. These super-sized gold discs make a standard cabinet much more interesting. When coupled with a larger-than-expected bedside lamp the ensemble makes an eye-boggling focal point.

final details
knobs and handles

One of the easiest ways to change the look of your furniture is with new knobs and handles. Some involve spending huge bucks, but others are unpardonably cheap and all can be installed in the blink of an eye (page 84). Before deciding whether to opt for handles or knobs you'll need to take into account the weight of the door or drawer – heavy loads need handles to distribute the weight more effectively. Otherwise, there's no need to worry about restraint: go for all-out daring and razzle-dazzle.

Glass and crystal are great options if you are looking for a shimmering, glamorous glow. Classic yet contemporary, they work well against most other textures and in almost any design scheme.

Brushed or polished nickel, with its silvery white sheen, adds an interesting layer of texture to any surface. If your home is quite minimalist, then a simple treatment of brushed nickel might just do the trick. The polished version is rather architectural in feel and will create an immediate modern vibe.

Antique-style bronze is classic, traditional and timeless. Handles and knobs can be rather weighty in look and are among the more costly options, although modern repro versions can be found more cheaply.

Other materials each bring their own contribution to style. For a walk on the wild side consider leather – uber-glamorous, unique and dressy. Knobs made from coloured resin, which is available in a plethora of psychedelic colours, will add a funky, artistic touch. Ceramic handles lend a softer, hand-made look to your décor, while natural wood also gives a gentler face lift.

Themed knobs and handles, such as vegetable or celestial shapes (the list is endless), are a tongue-in-cheek alternative, which can be utilized to tie in with your décor – or provide a startling contrast. They are not always expensive and can be found in many regular hardware stores.

These elongated door handles on the wardrobe really play around with scale. Over-sized and confident, they provide a striking embellishment to otherwise featureless wardrobe doors. And using old bus signs in a wall collage is certainly a 'one in a million' idea!

how to...
fit door handles

Handles can make a fundamental difference to the overall design of furniture. Think of smooth oak cut into outsized strips, the perfect way to turn monotonous doors into something eye-catchingly chic.

shopping list

wood of choice
sandpaper
wood adhesive
nails
hammer
paint or vanish
paint brush
carpenter's pencil
variable-speed drill plus bits
screws
screwdriver
spirit level

1 Select the wood you require and get it cut at a DIY store into three pieces for each handle: a long piece for the handle itself and two short pieces for the ends. The long piece needs to be cut at 45 degrees at each end, the two smaller bits at 45 degrees at just one end to create mitre joints.

2 Sand down any rough edges (page 184) and glue together the three pieces that make each handle. Wipe off any excess adhesive. When dry nail them top and bottom for extra strength, making sure that the shaft of the nail goes down the length of the handle where it will not be seen. Paint or varnish as desired.

3 Decide on the position of the handle on the door. Mark a hole for drilling on the back of the door where the top of the handle will be. Drill the hole (page 181) from the back all the way through to the front of the door. Now drill a hole through the centre of the end piece at the top of the handle.

4 Screw the top of the handle lightly to the door from the back (page 181). Using a spirit level to make sure the door handle is perpendicular, mark the position of the bottom hole and drill all the way through the door and into the end piece of the handle. Screw into place firmly, and go back to tighten up the top screw. Repeat as necessary for further handles.

TOP TIP: There is plenty of scope for handle design, from the material used to the shape you create. Just be sure to make a bold visual statement.

colour

the effects of colour

Clever, clever colour. Used correctly, colour not only transforms a faceless room into something spectacular but it can also change our perceptions of its actual shape and size. In addition, each shade has its own psychological quality, so when choosing your palette bear in mind the effect you want to create – warm, cool, spacious, intimate (page 96). Colour behaves in three basic ways: passive, neutral and active. Passive colours are pale and subdued, making rooms feel airy and expansive. Neutral colours, such as white, cream and taupe, offer a great canvas in which to frame things like a stunning piece of furniture. And active colours are typically darker and warmer, creating a more intimate feel. Getting it right isn't rocket science: follow some basic rules and you'll go to the top of the class.

Painting walls the colour of sunshine generates warm energy in this dark hallway, and opting for a darker-than-usual tone creates an even more dramatic effect. Teamed with dark chocolate cornicing and a sky-blue ceiling, it is a marriage made in heaven.

the effects of colour
light and neutral

Whites, off-whites and neutrals create the illusion of space, so they are fabulous for use in small rooms. Restful and calm, they stay quietly in the background, making them ideal for bedrooms – and, if you love the serenity, almost any other room as well. Nothing if not versatile, neutrals will make any strong architectural features, such as cornicing, a ceiling rose or a fireplace, really stand out. Simplicity is very much the order of the day, but rooms can quite easily appear bland, dull and rather unfriendly. So consider varying the tonality of the colours (page 94), as well as creating an interplay of pattern (page 110) and texture to enliven your scheme.

A neutral palette creates the perfect atmosphere for this bedroom: light, breezy and relaxing. The simple curtains and bedding echo the elegant, feminine feel, while a touch of pattern in the wallpaper gives visual interest. Even the books on the windowsill add a touch of life and their very own smidge of colour.

see also:
texture p122

the effects of colour
dark with accents

If you're toying with going dark but haven't yet done so then go for it! Bold, inviting and elegant, dark colours transform a shy flower of a room into a head-turner. Don't think twice about enveloping your walls, floor and ceiling in the same intense shade: it will help blur the joins between them. For visual variation, combine different tones of the same colour (page 94), or accent the woodwork, furnishings or accessories with a strong, contrasting note – even small rooms can take four dark walls and a ceiling as long as you do this. The trick with accent colours is to vary the intensity and shade from the background colour. Then they will help define and enrich any dark space.

Walls have gone all grown up! Dark, smoky colours bring sophistication in both this kitchen and fireplace nook. The accent colours (the hot pink of the lettering, the acid yellow of the pear) add a dash of panache, making these spaces much more than just somewhere to cook or hang out – they become a statement in their own right.

see also:
planning p24

TOP TIP: A circular table in a kitchen is an ideal counterpoint to the straight lines of cabinets.

the effects of colour
tones and shades

When it comes to painting our homes we are often a little fearful about moving away from a neutral palette. We needn't be. For fabulous results all you need to do is familiarize yourself with a colour wheel (available from most art shops and on the Internet) and decide on a tonal, harmonious or complementary scheme. A tonal scheme uses either various shades of one colour, or more than one colour but all with the same intensity. Harmonious colours sit near or next to each other on the colour wheel and give a well-balanced, unified scheme. Complementary colours contrast (but don't clash); dramatic and daring, they are generally used in moderation for accents. Now you're ready to take the plunge!

Tonal schemes can look beautifully sophisticated, as they subtly graduate shades of one colour (monochromatic) or use more than one colour but with the same tone. There are no hard and fast rules about which colours to select, but the key to making this look work is to use plenty of texture and pattern to alleviate blandness. A trick many designers use is to take one colour and paint the ceiling in the lightest shade, the walls the next shade darker and the woodwork in the darkest.

Harmonious schemes use colours that sit next to or very close to each other on the colour wheel. The wheel's construction is rather simple: the three primary colours (red, yellow and blue) form its core. Three secondary colours (orange, green and purple) are created by mixing two of the primary colours together. Rounding out the colour wheel are the six tertiary or intermediate colours. These are made by mixing primary colours with secondary colours, for example, green and yellow to make lime. All of these colours can be mixed with one another to give an enormous array of hues, shades and tints. Harmonious schemes are the easiest for a DIY novice to use as the colour combinations are automatically pleasing to the eye.

Complementary schemes are bolder and far more dramatic than harmonious schemes. They use colours that are opposite each other on the wheel, which have strong visual resonance when they are placed alongside each other (for example, red teamed with green, or plum and yellow). When using complementary schemes, decide which colour you want to feature most – if you use all the colours in equal amounts they will fight for attention. You can also balance them out by introducing a few neutral colours (page 91), say, soft creams or whites.

see also:
texture p122

Tonal

This is a very balanced set of colours, whose dense hues all display a similar depth of tone. Used alone, any one of these would firmly anchor a space, but when put together, deep grey, blue, warm browns and plum set each other off beautifully.

Harmonious

A palette of light, breezy shades, from chalk to lilac, turquoise to blush, evokes a summer landscape. Muted and soft, they sit close to each other on the colour wheel and easily blend together, though they can also stand alone.

Complementary

Ideal for adding a finishing flourish, these intense shades occupy opposite places on the colour wheel. Vibrant cherry red, burnt orange and groovy deep blues and greens have great personality and really pile on the charm.

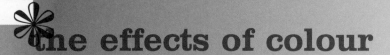

the effects of colour
colour moods

Figuring out the right colours to combine can be a daunting task – you want your room to look stunning but the choice is so vast! It is well known that colours have a psychological effect, so first think about the mood you want to create: warm and cosy or cool and calming. Certain colours affect the natural light; others enhance or diminish space, so be guided by the qualities of the room itself. With these considerations in mind you'll have the confidence to create a truly individual scheme.

Warm colours, such as reds, oranges and yellows, give a room a healthy glow and so are good in north- and east-facing rooms, where the natural light is at its weakest. Think oodles of burnt sienna with some damson, raspberry and pink thrown in. Loved by fashionistas, such colours ooze charm, but their deeper hues can gobble up sunshine – be sure to opt for some reflective finishes to bounce the light around. Warm colours tend to make surfaces appear closer (known as 'advancing'), making them fab for large hallways and for creating intimate dining rooms or boudoir-type bedrooms.

Cool colours like lilacs, greens and blues are ideal for west- and south-facing rooms as they tone down strong sunlight. They have the effect of making surfaces recede, enhancing the feeling of space, and are thus ideal in small areas. Soft and subtle, cool palettes are often thought of as relaxing, instilling an air of peace and tranquillity in bedrooms and studies. And even their deeper hues (strong electric blue, for example) will have the same effect.

Good combinations are harder to define, since there are no set rules. Be guided by mood. One of my favourite colour palettes is nutmeg, stone, pink, pecan and chocolate. Another is bronze, azure, deep grey, pearly white, salmon, buff, ochre and sage. Both are rich in feel, give a strong finish and can be used to create a sense of drama. But you might prefer a fresher look, so opt for colours that are clean and pure, such as lime, primrose and hot pink.

Bad combinations occur when rooms lack visual harmony, rather than when any particular colour no-nos are used – after all, colour choice is extremely personal and one girl's idea of colour heaven is another girl's psychedelic nightmare. So rather than avoiding specific combinations of colours, consider highlighting one shade and reducing the amount or intensity of the other. Moderation is the key: both under-stimulation (lack of variation in colour and tone) and over-stimulation (too many high-intensity contrasts) will have you swiftly running for the exit.

see also:
light p154

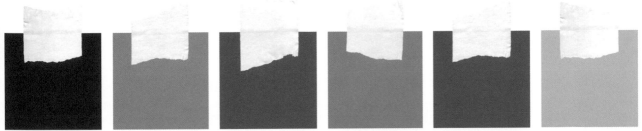

Warm colours

With its strong pigments of intense yellow, nutmeg and tangerine, as well as tones of red, this palette is welcoming and cheerful and works wonderfully when used over large, expansive areas like walls.

Cool colours

Subtle muted greens and blues make a powerful decorating tool as they can make surfaces appear to recede. Evoking the many shades of the sea, the palette is clear, fresh and inherently modern.

Colours that work together

These colours have an affinity as they are based on nature itself: baked earth, natural wood, pale stone, petrol blue, evergreen forests. One of many workable combinations, this palette has enough variation to keep the mix interesting.

*room analysis

Lots of colours together can be exhausting, so keep the palette for restful spaces simple and restricted.

Space Minimal furniture makes a room appear more spacious, helping it to feel lighter and calm.

Lighting Using a floor lamp rather than a traditional bedside table lamp allows more light to be distributed throughout the room.

Glamour Since the rest of the decorating scheme is plain, it is left to the unconventional door handles to add the wow factor.

Colour A unifying shade on the walls and wardrobes makes furniture unobtrusive. Harmony is maintained by painting floor and door trims the same colour.

Texture Adding a throw and over-sized cushions is an easy and stylish way to soften the room and create visual variation.

adding colour with paint
types of paint

A coat of paint can glamorize dull walls, make floorboards hip and breathe new life into tired furniture – there's simply no quicker or cheaper way to transform your home. Choosing the paint for the job is a matter of preference, although some suit specific areas better than others: generally, the higher the sheen the more durable the paint. One-coat paints speed things up but don't work as well for dark colours. Rolling, brushing and spraying are our choices when it comes to applying paint, each creating their own effect.

Emulsion is a water-based paint and has either a matt finish (which absorbs the light) or a silk sheen. It is perfect for hiding wall imperfections and also very good for ceilings, but becomes a bad option in bathrooms and kitchens as its porous surface absorbs dirt and water.

Eggshell paint can be oil- or water-based and has a very slight shine – picture the low sheen of an egg. It cleans up better than emulsion, so it is great on walls and woodwork alike.

Satin paint has more of a velvety shine. Often used for ceilings and woodwork, it will give well-plastered walls a lustrous look. Its oil-based formula holds up to light cleaning.

Gloss paint is also oil-based and is the most durable, its high sheen reflecting the most light. Easy to clean and water-resistant, it is great for woodwork and furniture. It is not a finish for walls, as it will highlight every blemish.

Textured paint contains sand or beads and is far thicker on application than ordinary paint. It is excellent for covering cracks and small imperfections and can turn ordinary walls into something more interesting.

Rollers are easy to use and to clean. They generally make the job faster, especially over large surfaces, but create more splattery mess. You will still need a brush at the joins with the ceiling and door, and the finish will have a slight 'orange peel' appearance.

Brushes give you great control, make less mess and are essential for a fine application of paint in hard-to-reach places. Quality paint brushes make a huge difference to the end result. Think of them as you do make-up brushes and go with natural bristles, which hold the paint better than synthetic ones and are also much more flexible, enabling a smoother application.

Spraying gives a fine professional finish but should be reserved for small items such as pieces of furniture and picture frames. It's a messy business and so is best done outdoors.

This lively and intense combination of colours gives a thoroughfare maximum impact. The strong red wall colour is sufficiently toned down and contained by using a complementary dark brown shade for the door frame and cornicing.

how to...
paint walls

Paint is a great way to spruce up walls without blowing the budget. Rollers are a quicker way of working but your finish will be much smoother if you use a good-quality brush.

shopping list

protective sheets
stepladder
sugar soap
sponge
all-purpose filler (if required)
plaster sealer
masking tape
white emulsion
paint
paint stirrer
selection of paint brushes

1 Cover the floor and furniture with protective sheets and strip off previous wallpaper thoroughly (page 183). Wash walls with sugar soap (page 184) and fill cracks or holes with an all-purpose filler (page 183). Prime bare walls with a plaster sealer to prevent them from absorbing too much paint.

2 Mask off woodwork, light switches, fireplaces and so on (page 180) and apply a layer of watered-down emulsion to act as a base coat. (If you are painting a pale colour over an existing dark one then do not dilute the emulsion.) Allow to dry for the time recommended in the manufacturer's instructions.

3 Ensure you have enough paint for the job (different batches may vary in colour) and stir well with a paint stirrer or stick (page 181). Using a 37mm brush held at an angle, paint a narrow band all around the edges of the wall where it meets the ceiling, skirting and other walls, as well as light switches and so on (known as 'cutting in'). Keep a firm, steady hand to give yourself a good straight edge.

4 Now switch to the biggest brush you feel comfortable with (75mm is a good size) and paint the rest of the wall one section at a time, working from right to left and away from any windows. Maintain a flowing vertical action with your wrist, turning the brush to go over again and smooth out. Avoid overloading the brush with paint as this will result in splashes and runs.

5 Try to catch any runs as they happen. If they have already dried you will need to lightly sand off and then re-coat. Paint outwards over the edge of any external corners and always finish a wall before taking a break or your joins will show.

6 Allow the paint to dry for the recommended time and apply a second coat as before. Clean your brushes thoroughly when finished (page 180).

2

TOP TIP: Safety first: take care that you do not overreach when working on a stepladder.

adding colour with paint
painted floors

Extending the canvas of the room beyond the walls and ceilings, painted floors give a whole other vibe to modern living. On the practical side, they are super-easy to paint (page 106) and simple to maintain. Carpets may well be warm and soft to lie on, but they aren't great for allergy sufferers, quickly go out of fashion and won't last as long as floorboards. And think of this: painted floors actually improve with age! Even when beaten up and scuffed with wear and tear, that so-in-vogue soft, weathered patina will never go out of style.

Painting floors dark and glossy instantly turns them from standard to sophisticated. Beautifully reflective, it is the perfect way to spruce up a staircase and also creates a wonderful surface against which to highlight something as fabulous as this quirky canine sculpture and decorative lampshade.

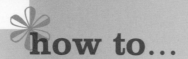

how to...
sand and paint floors

Remedy bland floors for ever by transforming your boards with a luxurious lick of paint – low cost, high impact! As ever, the key to a truly fabulous finish is in the preparation.

shopping list

industrial and rotary edge floor sanders
selection of grades of sandpaper
nail punch
hammer
masking tape
goggles and face mask
sugar soap
sponge
lint-free cloth
white spirit
knotting solution
wood primer
undercoat
paint
paint stirrer
selection of paint brushes

TOP TIP: Remember to start painting at the furthest point from the door to allow yourself an easy exit!

necessary to keep a slow, steady pace. Tilt the machine backwards when stopping and starting and, most importantly, keep it moving when it is switched on or it will gouge the boards.

3 Now change to the rotary sander and fit it with the coarse sandpaper. Work carefully around the edges of the room where the large sander did not reach. Take care not to damage skirting boards and doors.

4 Fit the large sander with medium-grade paper but this time work up and down the length of the boards, again overlapping each strip slightly. Switch to the edge sander using the same grade of paper. Finally, working with the fine grade paper, sand the length of the boards once more, repeating with the edge sander as before.

5 Vacuum the floor, sugar soap the boards and wipe over with a cloth dampened with white spirit to ensure it is completely dust-free (page 184). Mask off skirting boards and doorframes (page 180) and prepare the new wood for painting with knotting solution and a primer (page 183). Follow with a layer of undercoat (page 184).

6 Stir the paint thoroughly (page 181) and start to paint in the corner the furthest away from the door, using the largest brush you feel comfortable with, but not one that is wider than the boards themselves (a 75mm brush is a good size). Paint the whole length of one or two boards at a time, switching to a smaller brush (25mm) where the floor meets the skirting boards and walls to allow a finer application of paint.

7 When dry, lightly sand by hand, vacuum and wipe as before, and apply a second coat. Paint doesn't reach its full hardness until three to four days afterwards, so avoid excessive wear and tear on the area. Clean your brushes thoroughly after use (page 180).

1 Sanding floorboards is a messy old job but fundamental to the best results. You will need to hire an industrial floor sander and a smaller rotary sander for the edges, as well as three grades of sandpaper: coarse, medium and fine. First tap down any protruding nails to just below the surface with a nail punch and hammer. Small gaps between boards add character, but if you are worried about bigger gaps then glue in narrow pieces of wood to fill. Seal around the door with masking tape (page 180).

2 Fit a coarse sheet of sandpaper to the sander (your machine will come with instructions), put on your goggles and face mask and sand in diagonal strips across the floor, overlapping slightly to ensure good coverage. The machine will move of its own accord when switched on, so some restraint will be

how to...

paint doors

Give your doors a lick of paint and they'll soon be looking their glossy, glamorous best. A few tricks of the trade are all you need for a professional finish.

shopping list

stepladder
protective sheets
masking tape
sandpaper
knotting solution
wood primer
sugar soap
sponge
lint-free cloth
white spirit
undercoat (if required)
selection of paint brushes
eggshell or gloss paint

1 Cover the floor with protective sheets, remove all door furniture and mask off where the doorframe meets the wall (page 180). Lightly sand new wood for painting and apply knotting solution followed by a primer (page 183). Doors that have been painted before can simply be sanded and sugar soaped (page 184). However, if there are lots of lumps and bumps then it is best to completely strip the door first (page 183). Wipe down with a lint-free cloth dampened with white spirit to remove any debris.

2 Apply a layer of undercoat with a 50mm brush to prevent it absorbing too much of the paint. (A pale topcoat requires a pale undercoat; if you are going dark then your undercoat must also be dark.) When dry, lightly sand and wipe down as before.

3 To apply paint to a flat door select a flat brush and work in small sections from the top left-hand corner across and down, overlapping by a third to avoid misses. Work with a smooth wrist action that follows the grain of the door and never overload the paintbrush. Don't over-brush the paint or it will lose its shine. Brush out runs quickly with an upward stroke.

4 For panelled doors start with the panels first, working from the inside outwards, then change to a 50mm angled brush for the mouldings. Lastly paint the flat areas with the flat brush, starting with the inner verticals, then the horizontals and lastly the two long outer verticals. You will need to work quickly between painting all the aspects of the door, blending in the joins between sections as you go.

5 Lastly, paint the doorframe with the smaller angled brush. Standard oil-based paints need 24 hours to dry before a second coat can be applied. Clean your brushes thoroughly when you have finished (page 180).

TOP TIP: Don't slash the budget on paint brushes – the better the brush, the better the finish.

adding colour with pattern

Decorating with pattern as well as with colour is a surefire way of creating a highly individual design. So if your room seems a tad bland with just paint, then consider introducing some element of pattern, whether through wallpaper, furniture or accessories like rugs and cushions. Start off by being as adventurous as you can, remembering that rooms can easily take up to six or seven different combinations without looking too crazy. Generally speaking, it's good to use a variety of both pattern and scale – a large stripe juxtaposed with, say, a small floral pattern. Or choose designs from a similar theme, Chinoiserie or botanical prints, for example, to bring your look together. Colour is a cohesive factor, too, so opt for similar shades in each pattern to help with the unity of the overall scheme.

A multitude of different patterns side by side is high-impact stuff! Opulent and at the same time more than a touch whacky, it works because all the patterns draw on a unifying palette of raspberry tones, blues and greens, which is kept in check with some classic neutrals. It's not for the faint-hearted but it is spirited, enriching and certainly different!

TOP TIP: Space-enhancing concave mirrors prevent highly patterned décor from being too 'off the wall'.

adding colour with pattern
accents and moods

A combination of patterns works best when the eye is allowed to rest: too much visual stimulation is tiring and won't allow you to dally long in the room. Be sure to intersperse your design with some plainer notes to help highlight the patterns you have selected. So consider breaking it up with white woodwork and accessories, or setting your furnishings against a dark tone on the walls. Or just feature pattern in your accent items, like cushions, throws and rugs, which you can easily move around or remove entirely if it all gets too much. Pattern, like colour, will dictate the mood, so if you want something formal, opt for a sophisticated toile fabric or an in-fashion flock wallpaper; for something softer and more romantic, think billowing floral curtains. Exciting stuff!

The period picture and more modern upholstered rocking chair introduce pattern in quite different, yet complementary, ways. Together they make a strong graphic statement. The contrasting fabrics covering the chair really punch up the room and are beautifully balanced by the white painted floors and strong grey walls.

room analysis

Colour is back in fashion, with hot, funky shades combining with traditional ones to create a really individual look.

Style An assortment of picture frames prevents the design from looking too regimented.

Space Placing small-scale furniture in a large room with tall ceilings heightens the sense of grandeur.

Colour Taking a colour from the wallpaper and replicating it in your furniture and accessories results in a well-integrated look. Neutral skirting helps to frame the overall scheme of highly coloured rooms.

Texture A wildly patterned, highly textural rug in crazy colours works when used in isolation, as it is counterbalanced by the dark, glossy floor.

adding colour with pattern
types of wallpaper

Back in vogue in a big way, wallpaper is all about making a statement. Advances in modern technology mean that the choices of colour, pattern and surface texture are vast: you name it, you can get it. Prices range from cheap to stratospheric, meriting some careful consideration, but at least you can cut costs by hanging it yourself (page 118). So whether you want to cover the whole room or just a feature wall, wallpaper embellishes your walls like nothing else.

Lining paper is useful for disguising imperfections in walls or for hiding a previously applied strong colour. This is not a finished paper – it is merely the first layer before hanging the patterned wallpaper. However, it will take a coat of paint if your walls are not suitable for painting directly.

Pulp paper, the kind found in DIY stores, is cheap and easy to hang, with a pattern printed onto the basic paper. Although it is a good budget option and some designs are now quite imaginative, it is generally too thin to cover serious defects in the wall.

Woodchip was once considered a great option for disguising any lumps and bumps. However, it has few, if any, merits in terms of texture or style and can be a nightmare to strip off from walls at a later date.

Vinyl paper has a water-resistant coating on the face of the paper, making it extremely hard-wearing and ideal for humid environments like kitchens and bathrooms. It is easy to wipe down but its shiny surface is not to everyone's taste.

Anaglypta is an uncoloured, embossed paper with patterns ranging from light to heavily embossed and from floral to geometric. It is good for hiding defects in the wall but will require a coat or two of paint to finish.

Embossed paper has a raised, coloured design. Like Anaglypta, it adds a textural element to your design but, as it is the finished article, it doesn't need any painting.

Flock papers are incredibly tactile and very much back in fashion. The raised pattern is formed by powdered fibres, making the paper look and feel like velvet. Typical designs are large and floral (think paisley or damask), giving a room a more formal, luxurious tone.

Specialist papers are so numerous they can be hard to categorize. Hand-blocked papers have a body and depth of colour that cannot be matched by machine printing, but since they are made-to-order by artisans they come with a hefty price tag. Others include materials such as felt, leather, hessian, silk and grass for the ultimate textural feel!

Papering the walls in an unexpected bold print transforms this small hallway into a dramatic space, turning the walls into a work of art.

TOP TIP: Think outside the box and use every inch of space. A bar on a hallway table – why not?

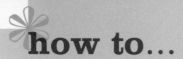

how to...

hang wallpaper

A few (must-have) tools and a little bit of elbow grease are all that's required to turn plain jane walls into the belle of the ball. By using the right equipment and sticking to the rules, your life will be easier and your walls will get a stunning personality.

shopping list

protective sheets
stepladder
scraper/filling knife
all-purpose filler
   (if required)
all-in-one primer-sealer
roller brush
wallpaper of choice
pasting table
retractable tape measure
long-bladed scissors
straightedge
wallpaper adhesive
pasting brush
pasting tray/bucket
sponge
plumb line
carpenter's pencil
paperhanger's brush
screwdriver
small cutting tool

1 Cover the floor and furniture with protective sheets and ensure that the walls are thoroughly stripped (page 183) Fill any cracks and holes and prepare the walls with a primer-sealer using a roller (page 184). (If you are hanging light-coloured paper on a darker wall then use a pigmented primer-sealer matched to the paper's background colour.) Allow at least 24 hours to dry.

2 Measure the length of paper required and cut from the roll, adding an extra 50mm at the top and bottom for final trimming. If using patterned paper, check that it is the correct way up – the outside end of the roll is not always the top. Ensure that there will be a complete motif at the top of the wall. Unroll the next length and check the pattern matches up before cutting. If the design is large or the repeat big, keep any off-cuts for smaller areas above windows and doors.

3 Turn your first length face down on the table and brush the wallpaper adhesive evenly downwards and out towards the edges, wiping off any that gets on the surface of the paper immediately with a damp sponge. If you are using pre-pasted paper, brush on water from a bucket or water tray in the same manner. Fold the paper in on itself from top to centre and from bottom to

centre, and leave to soak (the instructions on the adhesive will tell you how long).

4 When hanging bold patterned papers, start with a dominant wall (for example, a chimney breast) and plan to hang from its centre. If your paper is plainer then begin in a corner, working from left to right. Walls are rarely truly square so you will need to make a vertical pencil mark the width of your paper using a plumb line. Starting from the top, allow the plumb to freely swing until it rests, then mark at several points down the wall behind the string. Join up with a straightedge.

5 Open the top fold of paper and lightly stick the top half of the length to the wall, lining up the right side with your marked vertical line. Leave 50mm at the top of the wall for trimming. Smooth down the middle with a paperhanging brush, working out towards the edges to remove air. Open the lower fold and continue as before to the bottom. Wipe off any excess paste with a sponge. Run the tip of the scissors along where the wall meets the ceiling and floor. Slowly pull the length away and cut off the excess along this line. Brush back into place. When you come to hang the next piece, match the pattern with the previous length.

①

②

{ **TOP TIP:** For persistent air pockets, make a tiny incision with a cutting tool, expel the air and carefully stick down again. }

6 Never wrap a full width of paper around an inside corner – always do it in two pieces. First measure the distance between the edge of the last piece you hung and the corner at several points between ceiling and floor. Cut the paper along its length so that it is about 25mm wider than this measurement, paste and hang with the extra amount wrapping round the corner. Now paste the remaining length, and mark a vertical guide line on the next wall, a little more than the paper's width out from the corner. Hang parallel to the vertical line, brushing back into the corner and overlapping slightly with the 25mm already carried round. Match the pattern as best as you can. With outside corners use exactly the same technique, allowing a wrap-around of at least 50mm.

7 When papering around a door or window frame, cut the piece roughly to shape, leaving 25mm for trimming. Brush the paper into place alongside the frame, then score with the scissors and trim as before. This technique can be adapted for radiators and other fixed objects in the room. To paper around switches, first smooth the wallpaper down over the fitting. Pierce the paper and, for square shapes, make diagonal cuts using a small cutting tool from the centre of the switch to about 25mm beyond each corner; for circular switches, make a series of cuts like a star shape. Turn off the mains electricity supply and partially unscrew the fitting. Press the wallpaper firmly around where the fitting sits and trim away the surplus. Re-screw the fitting and switch the mains supply back on.

texture

creating texture

Texture brings rooms to life – but without an interplay of different fabrics and surfaces they can still seem staid and lacking in energy. The professionals fuse with aplomb, marrying leather with brick, silk with wool, raffia with glass. So aim for contrast: say, smooth floors with rough walls, grainy chenille cushions with velvet blankets, thick wool with thin muslin. Soft furnishings are the five-minute facelifts of the decorating world, instantly perking up your home with an array of different textures. They are also a room's ultimate indulgence: think the softest of merino wool throws, slub linen curtains, super-shiny satin cushions and worn leather pouffes. Increase the tactile possibilities by clustering in groups or leave as stand-alone statement pieces for additional emphasis – and arrange by theme, colour or scale.

Layers of textiles, accessories and personal mementos are like the jewellery of the room. Soft furnishings, such as throws and cushions, are by far the quickest way of adding texture, yet it is simple touches like these that make a room feel welcoming and complete.

✳ room analysis

Textiles that delight the skin – the most luxurious of wools, silks and cottons – are perfect for after-dinner lounging.

Window treatments The pairing of structural venetian blinds and warm, thick curtains adds another textural dimension.

Style Always layer: cushions on top of cushions and throws over sofas cook up warmth and cosiness.

Colour The exaggerated proportions of some of the furniture and the vibrancy of the colours don't overwhelm, since floors are kept neutral and pale.

Texture Furniture covered in a riot of fun fabrics is made far more informal. Using a hotch-potch of textures – thick, thin, shiny, dull – gives the space energy.

TOP TIP: A reflective metal splashback increases the feel of space by pushing back the walls.

creating texture

Texture is not just about the tactile – it's visual, too. And it is the surfaces in a room that will set the tone (page 128). Ceilings are a great starting point: they can be wallpapered, covered with textured paint or decorated with tiles. Walls can get roughed up by tongue-and-groove or even exposed brick for a bit of industrial chic. Floors could be skimmed with cement, covered in terracotta tiles for some country house charm, or laid with smooth, glossy hardwood for ultimate sophistication. Architectural features, such as dado rails, panelling and ceiling roses (page 132), add yet another textural layer to these surfaces and, depending on your choice, can even make a small room appear bigger or a larger room smaller. Mix and match your fabulous visual texture with a riot of fabrics and true magic occurs. It's that thrilling combination, both visual and tactile, that lends intrigue and vitality to any scheme. The only limit is your imagination!

This kitchen is decked with a range of different textures. Sheen is supplied by the brushed stainless steel splashback, the terracotta tiled floor, through to the glossy profiles of the appliances themselves. These shiny, hard-edged surfaces are relieved by the softness of the colourful upholstered armchair – a surprising element in a kitchen – and the warm wooden legs on the cabinets.

see also:
colour p110

surface texture
walls and floors

Texture can be introduced to a room in many ways, so deal first with the surfaces that make the framework of your room: the walls and floor. Certain finishes allow you to create different moods: concrete and brick provide a casual, New York boho kind of vibe, whereas wood panelling can add a warmer, more lived-in feel. But they do need to be paired carefully with the room's function, so a rough, pitted floor might not work so well in a kitchen, for instance, where it will be harder to keep clean. Panelling is the easiest technique to do yourself; the other applications require a lot of experience and are best left to the professionals – a major factor in the budget. Cost considerations aside, don't be afraid to experiment and choose your material accordingly.

Brick gives a raw, not-quite-finished edge to a room – but you'll never need to dust or clean it! You could consider exposing your walls to reveal the brick, if you have it, or create an 'inner skin' with bought-in bricks. Either of these will turn your home into a building site for a while, but an easier way to achieve the same effect is to fit brick tiles. Beautifully textural and available in a variety of colour palettes, from purply black through ochre yellow to the warmest orangey red, brick tiles take walls from the back row of the chorus to become the star of the show! And they work equally well on the floor, too.

Concrete is a surprisingly beautiful material, whether it is skimming floors or cladding walls. Highly decorative and favoured by interior designers the world over, it is now available in a whole host of colours and textures, helping you to create a truly unique look. Inherently industrial in feel, concrete can be made more homely by pairing it with softer accessories such as rugs and throws (page 122).

Plaster creates a whole other urban look. Bare, plastered walls are particularly amazing when hung with striking modern art or cool, glossy photographs, creating a juxtaposition of rough and smooth textures. Plaster can be coloured with a variety of tints (it is normally pale pink) and can be treated to all sorts of paint effects, from polished satin to trompe l'oeil murals.

Panelling, whether simple wooden plank panelling or tongue-and-groove, adds another visual layer to a room. It is useful for concealing bumpy walls and, if your rooms lack architectural features (page 132), then it will add much-needed character. Simple and elegant, it is relatively easy to fit yourself (page 130), making it a good option if your budget is limited.

Exposed brick walls are the rough diamonds of the decorating world. Worn, chipped and mismatched, this one certainly has a story to tell. When teemed with a bespoke tongue-and-groove stair banister and some sleek furniture, the effect is super-stylish.

how to...
fit tongue-and-groove panels

Whether painted the same colour as the rest of the room or accented with a pop-out colour, tongue-and-groove adds instant gravitas to your pad. It's also a good solution for imperfect walls that need covering up.

shopping list

tongue-and-groove
   panels
battens
wire brush
knife
variable-speed drill
   plus bits
wallplugs and screws
sandpaper
lint-free cloth
white spirit
spirit level
carpenter's pencil
panel pins
nail punch
hammer
finishing materials:
   knotting solution, wood
   primer, paint, varnish or
   wood stain
paint brush

1 Decide on the area to be covered by tongue-and-groove and have your panels and battens cut to size at a DIY store. Unwrap the timber, lay it flat on its side and leave in the room where it is to be fitted for at least two weeks in order to acclimatize. (This is long-winded but essential as wood absorbs moisture and can shrink or warp.)

2 Remove picture hooks, rails and sockets/light switches (remembering to turn off the mains electricity first). Wire brush the wall and hack off any crumbling plaster with a knife.

3 Attach battens horizontally to the wall at approximately 400mm intervals, using a drill, wallplugs and screws (page 181). You will need to drill the battens first, hold them up to the wall and mark the holes for drilling. For plaster walls use battens of 22 x 50mm, with screws 20mm longer than the combined thickness of the battens and plaster. For brick or blocks use battens of 38 x 50mm and fixings at least 60mm long.

4 Lightly sand the cladding and vacuum off any dust, then wipe over with a lint-free cloth dampened with white spirit (page 184). If you have any outside corners, begin there and work your way around the room. (You will need to have the boards mitred for a seamless joint.) Otherwise, start in the left-hand corner, and place the first tongue-and-groove panel against the wall, using a spirit level to make sure it is vertical. Drive a panel pin through the tongue and into each batten to secure, using a nail punch as you get closer to the board.

TOP TIP: If your wall is uneven pack out behind the battens with hardboard.

5 Slot the tongue into the groove of the next panel, tapping the new board into position with an off-cut piece of wood and hammer. Secure with panel pins as before. For an inside corner you simply butt the two panels together (you may have to have the last panel cut to the necessary width). If you are not covering the full height of the wall, use a dado or shelf to complete the look.

6 You will need to have holes cut in the boards for light switches and sockets. Get a qualified electrician to bring them forward to the new level of the wall. Finish with knotting solution, wood primer, paint, varnish or wood stain.

surface texture
architectural features

If your home has any architectural features whatsoever, then cherish them. Homes built after the 1960s are often devoid of interesting ceiling roses, mantelpieces, elaborate banisters and the like, but thanks to modern reproductions and the prevalence of salvage yards, such details are no longer the province of period buildings. You don't have to be slavishly correct or overly opulent. A relatively simple moulding will do the same great job as a highly decorative one; even the humble skirting board can give character to modern, boxy rooms. Putting the elegance back through architectural elements will add a wonderful layer of texture to any space – and what's more, they are relatively cheap and easy to fit.

Coving is a concave moulding that runs around the tops of walls, at the junction with the ceiling. Traditionally made of plaster, modern designs are now available in lightweight polystyrene or paper-wrapped substances. Keep the width of the coving in balance with the space: the smaller the room, the narrower the coving.

Cornicing is similar to coving but is fixed to the ceiling and is generally more decorative. Accenting it in a contrasting colour to the walls and ceiling will make this moulding stand out.

Dado rails are usually placed about a third of the way up the wall and are great for small rooms as the horizontal trim really draws the eye around the space. They will also help to break up the expanse of a large wall, and are an ideal finish for tongue-and-groove panelling (page 130).

Picture rails, like dados, add interest and help protect walls, as you can attach picture hooks and nails to the rail without having to make holes in the wall itself. They are typically placed about one quarter of the way down the wall from the ceiling.

Ceiling roses add a beautiful focal point to any space, whether or not they surround a central light fitting. Fairly simple to install (page 134), they draw the eye upwards, making ceilings appear higher, and give sophistication to a plain room.

Mantelpieces are very much the focal point of a room, anchoring the space and bringing a wall to life, even if the fire iself isn't active. Designs vary from highly decorative cast iron, inset with period tiles, to the simplest of wooden structures. The mantel shelf is handy for displaying your treasures, too.

A period mantelpiece adds a traditional flourish to this bedroom, without compromising its contemporary, urban feel. The small cast-iron grate and its mantel are in keeping with the small-scale room, neither swamping it nor diminishing it.

see also:
glamour p62; p78
colour p92

TOP TIP: Hanging a feature light off-centre adds a boudoir vibe to any room.

how to...
put up a ceiling rose

Whether made from plaster, plastic or foam, a ceiling rose is a fab way of adding texture to your room. Even if you don't have a central light it can still make a stunning centrepiece.

1

2

{ **TOP TIP:** Ask for a little help from your friends with this particular job – it will be far easier, quicker and much more fun. }

shopping list

ceiling rose of choice
stepladder
cloth
plaster sealer and paint
   (if desired)
paint brush (if required)
stud finder (if required)
variable-speed drill
   plus bits
pencil
adhesive
screws
screwdriver
caulk
all-purpose filler
filling knife

1 If removing an existing light fitting, first turn off the mains electricity. Unscrew your fitting so that you are left with just the exposed wiring. (If you do not know how to disconnect and reconnect lighting then call an electrician.) Clean the ceiling by dusting and wiping with a damp cloth.

2 If you wish to paint the rose, do so now, ensuring that you first apply a coat of plaster sealer to plaster roses.

3 Heavy plaster roses need supporting with screws as well as glue, so locate your ceiling joists with a stud finder (page 181), hold up the rose and drill at several points around its edge through into the joists. Make a larger hole through the centre for the electrical cord. Lighter plastic or foam roses need only the centre hole.

4 Turn over the rose and apply the manufacturer's recommended adhesive all around the rim and on any other parts that will touch the ceiling.

5 Carefully climb the stepladder with the rose and rest it on the ladder while you thread the electrical cord through the centre hole. Now press the rose firmly to the ceiling to set in place. Screw plaster roses to the ceiling using the holes you made earlier, taking care not damage the rose by over-tightening.

6 When dried, caulk around the edges to fill any gaps with the ceiling and cover screw holes with all-purpose filler. Touch up with paint if necessary.

7 Attach your light fitting back to the wiring and turn the power supply back on for a truly electrifying finish!

room analysis

Texture turns a practical space into a sensual one. It's all about the contrast of surfaces: glossy with matt, rough with smooth.

Window treatments Formal, full-length curtains dress up and soften windows, without obscuring their form.

Colour The subdued palette of the walls allows stunning accessories like the antique mirror and side table to really stand out – yet the overall look remains calm.

Texture The lived-in vintage furniture has an inherent textural quality. Layering the chairs and sofas with textiles demarcates the seating areas and makes for an interesting composition.

Light Shiny polished floors amplify light, increasing the sense of space.

✳ flooring

Make no mistake: dingy, scratched floors, beaten-up lino and 1960s shagpile have to go. Contemporary flooring needs to feel fabulous underfoot and be sophisticated enough to take you from one decade to the next. Floors can handle almost any treatment, so choice is really determined by lifestyle, comfort and degree of use. If you lead a hectic life you really want a floor that needs very little maintenance, such as laminate. If you're a big fan of lounging then carpets or rugs are an obvious choice, giving a casual, more informal feel. Pets and children in the home require hard-wearing surfaces like floorboards, stone or tiles, which can nevertheless impart elegance and sophistication. Once you've taken all that into consideration, figuring out which flooring to go for should be almost easy, no?

An assortment of beautiful kelims makes a richly decorative stair runner (page 140), adding interesting elements of texture, colour and pattern. It instantly transforms these stairs into something extraordinary, lending warmth and softness to the staircase.

Vintage printed linoleum adds comfort and vibrancy to this bathroom. Wonderful to pad around on, it is both water-tolerant and warm underfoot. Over the 50 years of its lifetime the surface patina has taken on a whole new character.

see also:
colour p110

how to...

make an eclectic stair runner

Inject funkiness to your stairs with a mix-and-match approach! This highly individual runner gives a luxurious feel but, by using second-hand oddments, won't cost the earth.

shopping list

assortment of rugs
retractable tape measure
scissors
staple gun plus staples

1 Measure the width of your stairs and cut the rugs to approximately 75 percent of this figure.

2 Starting at the top of the stairs, place your fabric about 100mm over the landing floor and staple to the wood at approximately 50mm intervals with a staple gun.

3 Press the rug down over the first riser and tread, turning over the edges if necessary to prevent fraying. Secure along both edges at approximately every 100mm, stapling the rug to both tread and riser.

4 Repeat on subsequent steps until the fabric is nearly finished. Trim this rug so that it ends at the junction of the previous riser and tread. Now take the next rug, line up to make a tidy join and staple to secure. Repeat until you have reached the bottom of the stairs.

5 Trim the last rug so that it ends where the stairs meet the floor and staple at 50mm intervals for a neat finish.

TOP TIP: A staple gun is a great tool to have in your collection, handling a huge variety of jobs around the home quickly and safely.

flooring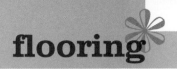

carpets, tiles and more

The floor is one of the largest surface areas in your home, so what goes down will determine the overall aesthetic. Cracking the code for flooring is not an easy task. With the multitude of options out there it really comes down to the usage the floor will receive – but not at the expense of a fabulous feel-good factor. These are big, scary decisions, often defined by budget, but get the flooring right and anything else you throw at your room will look fantastic.

Floorboards are the simplest of treatments yet have great warmth and sensuality. Whether varnished or painted, the light that reflects off them lends a glow to all other objects in the room. They are timeless, classic and hard-wearing, and any scuffs and knocks only serve to add character.

Laminate flooring mimics the look of hardwood but is cheaper to buy and easier to maintain. Great in high-traffic areas such as hallways, laminate is virtually resistant to scuffing, scratching and burns.

Vinyl and linoleum are extremely reasonable in cost and are available in a huge range of colours and styles. Whether from a roll or in individual tiles, they are super-easy to lay and replace. What's more they are dust- and water-resistant, and will last a lifetime.

Rubber flooring is no longer the stuff of schoolrooms. Now back in fashion with tons of choices available, it is a great option for home exercise spaces and children's rooms, as it requires virtually no maintenance and retains its sheen and colour for years.

Carpets and rugs soften harder surfaces, muffle noise and help balance rooms. Opt for wool wherever possible, as it outlasts all its synthetic counterparts and becomes more beautiful with age. Carpet tiles are useful, as only one or two tiles need to be replaced if there is any damage. Strategically placed rugs help break up a large area and can be a good budget option for disguising a worn-out floor.

Tiles are a great choice for bathrooms and kitchens since they are waterproof and easy to clean. Sealed cement, ceramic, porcelain and glass tiles all add a lovely visual rhythm as well as colour. Options range from the tiniest mosaics to large, geometric slabs.

Stone floors, such as marble, slate and granite, are also extremely durable and have an unparalleled wow factor, though they are frequently the most expensive option and need to be laid by a professional. Stone is cold to the touch, so it is worth considering under-floor heating, though this will add another costly element to the budget.

A contemporary sisal rug skims the polished wooden floor, giving a hard-wearing yet comfortable surface. Laying a smaller rug with a livelier pattern over the top adds additional texture, giving balance and vitality to this living room.

see also:
planning p20
colour p105

light

light up your life

Getting the right balance between natural light, functional lighting and its aesthetic aspects is essential in the design of any home. Yet all too often lighting is an afterthought in a decorating scheme. Assessing the amount of natural light should be the starting point. Window treatments need to be chosen, where possible, to maximize daylight, although strong sunshine may need to be tempered at different times of the day (page 151). In addition, each room needs a combination of three lighting types: general background or ambient lighting; task lighting, for working, reading or cooking; and feature or accent lighting (stunning decorative lights or ones that highlight structural features of a room). Layering is the watchword: mix and match a selection of pendant lights, recessed, table and floor lights, not to mention a smattering of candles and fairy lights, to create interesting lighting effects.

Feature lighting at its very best: over-sized contemporary wicker floor lights bathe the room in a soft, dappled glow. Playing with scale is the real trick to making this look work. Note how they have been teamed with smaller items like candles for balance.

light up your life
feature lighting

Scene-stealing feature lighting is approximately three times as bright as ambient or background lighting and produces focused, localized light. Whether traditional or modern in form, it gives shape and texture to your overall lighting scheme. You should aim to make a statement that stops people in their tracks but at the same time creates the right atmosphere. It requires all-out bravery: consider uber-glam chandeliers, over-sized floor lights or super-sophisticated table lights, with wondrous shades in hot colours like freesia yellow or Chinese peony red. Dimmers also produce astonishing results: rather than having a single level of illumination they allow you to create a whole range of tones, from muted and soft to dazzlingly bright.

A plethora of lamps here creates little nooks of interest and cosiness. But note how they are comparable in size and shed a similar amount of light, distributing small points of illumination evenly throughout the room. The long venetian windows are kept free of furniture and obtrusive curtains to allow natural light to flood in.

light up your life
filtering natural light

To dress or not to dress? Easily answered by beginning with some bare facts! If you have fabulous views and are not overlooked, then there really is no need to cover up your windows. Similarly, if your frames are architecturally interesting then leave them undressed for a cool style statement. Or you may prefer to filter the light with gauzy fabric such as voile or muslin, which will cut the glare but preserve the views (page 166). If, on the other hand, you want to frustrate nosy neighbours or block out strong sunlight, or need the room to be dark for sleeping, then select curtains, blinds (page 168) or shutters (page 171) to fit the job. Just remember that your window treatments should be in balance with the rest of your furnishings – a finishing flourish, if you like.

This simple sheer blind screens out the view but filters the daylight beautifully. Informal in style, its clean lines complement the rest of the scheme while the delicate pattern adds a welcome decorative note.

*room analysis

Unusual sculptural lighting and reflective surfaces make a bright room arresting, without drawing too much attention to individual elements.

Window treatments A decorative metal screen in front of the window is an unusual alternative to a blind, affording privacy whilst filtering the light. The undressed window fits in well with the lines of the room.

Lighting An assortment of lights, arranged asymmetrically around the perimeter of the room, create rhythms of light and shadow, bringing a sense of drama to the space.

Planning Placing seating around a central coffee table invites conversation.

Texture Glossy painted floorboards, the glass coffee table and highly polished screen multiply the effects of the light, as well as adding depth.

lighting effects

Light and reflection are your tools for creating a vibrant mood for a room. Reflective surfaces, from the glossiest of painted floors to mirrored tables, cause natural or artificial light to dance around the space, making it feel lively and interesting. They have space-enhancing qualities, too: glass-topped tables appear to float off the floor, while glossy lacquered or metal furniture makes a room feel larger than it really is. When light fittings are made of reflective materials themselves they can enliven dark corners by adding a shimmering glow, so experiment with psychedelic swirls of gold, mirrored glass or shiny steel. The savviest fittings are super-sized, but you need to maintain balance and control, so think of pairing over-sized lights with discreet wall-mounted fittings or delicate floor lamps, and make sure they relate to each other by a shared shape or material. It's called decorating with drama!

Strong, highly reflective surfaces dazzle and contrast in this dining room, creating pockets of intense light. The walls and ceiling may be dark but they are brought to life by the glossiness of the flamboyant furniture and super-scale lamp.

lighting effects
light fittings

Enter any lighting shop and you will be faced with an endless display of table lamps, floor lamps, recessed spots and pendants. So how to figure out which does what? It sounds a bit of a minefield with so many choices out there, but choosing a fixture for your home is relatively easy once you've figured out how it will actually distribute light. Remember that different shades and light bulbs (page 158) can affect the intensity and direction of the light, too, so don't be afraid to experiment.

Pendant lights, typically hung from a central point on the ceiling, only ever work if they are used in combination with other light sources, as they cast a dim, flat light and create harsh shadows. When fitted with a high-watt bulb they will turn your room into an interrogation cell quicker than you can say 'Geneva Convention' – use a dimmer so you can adjust the level of light appropriately. Pendant lights can provide a stunning decorative contribution, however, coming in a plethora of styles from drop-dead gorgeous venetian chandeliers to the simplest of paper lanterns.

Wall lights gently soften the light around the perimeter of the room so are perfect for providing ambient lighting. They work well in living rooms and in hallways, where floor space is at a premium.

Uplighters throw light onto the ceiling – great when the ceiling itself is painted in a light colour. Usually tall and thin, they take up little floor space and so can easily be placed behind large pieces of furniture or stashed in corners.

Downlighters are either recessed in the ceiling or surface mounted and cast directional light below. They are ideal for angling at kitchen and bathroom work surfaces, but unless boosted by other light sources can make the room gloomy and shop-like.

Floor and table lamps can be used in abundance, especially if you don't have ceiling lights. Floor lamps come in various styles, from the good old-fashioned standard lamp to more modern interpretations. Table lamps should be chosen with the size of the surface in mind or they will look top heavy. However, those placed on the floor can afford to be larger.

Anglepoise lamps have heavy bases and move freely in all directions. They are a good source of task lighting, and so are perfect in your home office or beside the bed.

This living room really comes alive with its combination of pendant, floor lights and candelabras. Swathed in vintage silks, the decorative lamps have all been given a similar treatment for a unifying effect.

lighting effects
light bulbs

Different light bulbs produce different kinds of light and so must be chosen to fit their purpose. A well-orchestrated combination of bulbs in a variety of light fittings will give you the most adaptability in your room, so think halogen for crisp, white light (fab for task lighting in kitchens) and tungsten for warm, yellowish light (creating super-sexy ambience in living rooms). But remember: never put a higher wattage in the fixture than recommended by the manufacturer and always buy the highest wattage allowed, giving you the flexibility to dim.

Tungsten or incandescent bulbs are your everyday household type, although they may eventually be phased out. The light they give off is yellowish and warm and, since they brighten warm colours and mute cooler ones, they are perfect for creating atmosphere and intimacy. Tungsten bulbs use mains electricity, don't need transformers, are readily available and are cheap to buy – although they have a short life span. The clear, pearl and coloured versions all give subtly different effects, but the clear ones tend to cast unsightly shadows.

Halogen bulbs produce a purer, sharper white light than tungsten as they burn at a much higher heat. Great in areas of activity such as kitchens and studies, they are available both in low voltage and mains voltage. (For low voltage you will need an in-built transformer or have one fitted to keep the wattage to 12 volts.) These bulbs make colours look crisper and, as they are slim and compact, are suited to either uplighters or downlighters.

Fluorescent bulbs, once associated with factory floors and office environments, have come a long way. There are literally hundreds of different types, each suitable for a different purpose, and what's more they are energy efficient and thus very economical. Since they give off very little heat they can be used in confined spaces. Available in curved or circular tubes, they are great for mini striplights, say in a kitchen.

Energy-saving bulbs work in the same way as a fluorescent tube. They cost less to run and also don't need to be replaced as frequently as standard light bulbs. They are available in various shapes and sizes – styles have recently become a lot more glamorous – although not all of them can be used with dimmers.

This large, decorative bulb dispels the myth once and for all that naked bulbs cast a nasty light. Whether in a clear or pearl finish, the globe emits a glorious glow and is as integral a part of the light fitting as its frame.

see also:
colour p96

how to...

spray paint a lamp

This simple technique can transform a tired old standard lamp into something way more playful and unconventional – yet it requires minimal effort from you.

shopping list

old standard lamp (or
   other junk shop find)
flattened cardboard box
   or protective sheet
small cutting knife
sandpaper
sugar soap
sponge
lint-free cloth
white spirit
overalls, goggles and
   face mask
electric paint sprayer
extension lead
oil-based paint

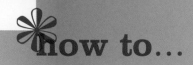

TOP TIP: Electric paint sprayers make the job much easier and give a more professional finish.

1 Spraying is a messy business and you need to avoid inhaling the spray, so find an outdoor location away from cars or garden furniture and cover the immediate area with a flattened cardboard box or protective sheet. A further box as a canopy is a good idea – the more localized you can make the spraying, the easier it will be to clear up after you have finished.

2 Strip any unwanted material from the lampshade (or other object) using a small cutting knife. Lightly sand painted or varnished areas, clean with sugar soap, then wipe down with a cloth dampened with white spirit (page 184).

3 Put on your overalls or your special decorating clothes (page 180), goggles and face mask, making sure you look your glamorous best. Load the paint sprayer with paint, following the manufacturer's instructions as to the amount of paint required and how much it should be diluted.

4 Hold the spray gun perpendicular to the surface of the object (holding it at an angle deposits paint unevenly) and move the paint sprayer over the surface at a steady rate. (Practise on some card beforehand if you feel unsure.) Don't be tempted to get too close: spraying from a short distance gives a thinner, more even coat, and you can always move closer to get better coverage if necessary. Try to overlap the paint as you go.

5 Your first coat won't be perfect. At least two coats are required for an even finish, but make sure you leave the recommended time for drying between applications. Clean the equipment thoroughly afterwards.

lighting effects
changing moods

Creating a bright mood for a room can be tricky, as it can easily become too garish. So forget about just flicking on that single pendant smack in the centre of the ceiling. The solution is to wash the room with ambient light as well as accenting particular features – even a daytime mood must have some shadow for contrast. Aim for a selection of different lighting (page 157) to bring out rich colours and designs. At the flick of a switch you need to be able to turn your home from a light, bright space into a cosy, shimmering pad. Think of placing lamps on lower levels as well as higher. Low-watt bulbs (page 158) cast a yellowy light, as do those that have been subdued by dimmers, making them ideal for intimate, evening moods. And by grouping candles in clusters you will create a softer layer altogether, setting the scene for seduction.

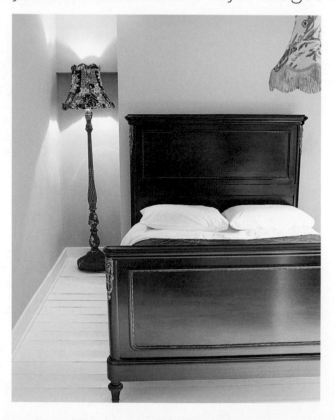

Washing the walls and ceiling with soft light creates just the right ambience, without making the rooms too gloomy. Decorative lighting draws the eye, creating an oasis of intimate light. The mood is seductive, yet cosy and tranquil.

*room analysis

Layered lighting creates the perfect ambience for evening entertaining: shadows in some corners are well balanced by pools of light in others.

Glamour Fairy lights strung over artwork draw the eye and add another layer of lighting to the overall design.

Colour A moody tonal scheme, coupled with lights placed at low levels, draws down the high ceiling, making the room feel cosier.

Lighting Lamps have been dimmed to varying levels, dappling the space with different colours and intensities of light. Groups of candles create pinpoints of flattering, flickering illumination.

Style Different types of furniture and lighting sit happily alongside one another and look inviting.

window treatments
curtains and voiles

Most fabrics can be used for curtains, so dress your windows according to the room's function. Gauzy voiles grant both privacy and light, while heavier materials provide warmth and seclusion. Opposites offer surprising contrasts, so pair lustrous velvet over shimmering taffeta or huge banners of linen with colourful silks behind. And remember , the length of the curtain makes a huge difference: short says informal, long shouts show-stopping party gown. The number of headings (the gathering at the top of the curtain) is never-ending – the principal ones are listed below – but they can define the curtain's style. Equally, the choice of pole and tracking should be part of the design.

Pencil pleats are the most popular, with tidy folds running consistently across the curtain, looking rather like a row of pencils, in fact. They are fab for lightweight or sheer fabrics.

Pinch, French or triple pleats are small clusters of folds, grouped at regular intervals. Opt for these for heavy full-length curtains as they bunch well, creating less bulk at the sides.

Gathered pleats are a cross between pinched and pencil and are best for short, lightweight curtains. They work particularly well for striped or checked material as they condense the pattern at the top.

Goblet pleats are by far the most formal, with stiff, cylindrical cuffs that have been filled with interlining to create a three- or four-pronged pleat – a classic style ideal for large patterns.

Tab tops have loops made from the same or contrasting fabric and can only be used with curtain poles. They look good with heavy, plain material and result in fewer but deeper folds in the curtain.

Eyelet or rivet headings have a modern, slightly industrial feel and, again, can only be used with poles. They are great for use with thicker fabrics like suede or leather, which do not easily fold.

Tracking ranges from plain old plastic to uber-cool metal and is available in various diameters. If you have an awkward-shaped window, then select aluminium tracks as these can be moulded, allowing your fabric to follow the contours.

Poles, like tracks, are available in different sizes and can be made from a variety of materials such as brass or bamboo. An unobtrusive alternative is to opt for steel tension wires. The caps at the end of the pole are called finials, and designs for these vary from subtle to ornate.

These delicate curtains highlight the frame of the window without swamping it, while the translucent lace gently filters the natural light. Simply hung, they hint at romance without resorting to excessive swags and frills.

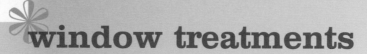

window treatments
blinds

Roller, roman or venetian? Wooden or metal? A big old conundrum – but one that can easily be sorted. The rule of thumb is that whatever you select should be in harmony with the rest of the room: if you consider blinds as a final touch rather than a starting point you won't go far wrong. And if you haven't finished decorating yet, you can always opt for the simplest solution – say, a white roller blind – and add a more elaborate layer later on.

Roller blinds are cheap, practical and utterly simple. They can be cut to size, so are useful for even the smallest window. Rollers are fab if you have a great view that shouldn't be covered up, as they can completely disappear at the top of the frame. If privacy isn't required, select thin weaves such as muslin or voile that gently filter the light. And if you're after something more fancy, rollers can be easily embellished with pom-poms, fringing, rings, tassels or beads.

Roman blinds form loose, horizontal pleats when raised and hang flat when lowered. They are ideal if you want a more decorative window treatment but don't have the room for curtains. Choose a really cool pattern and they act like a piece of art, adding an immediate zing to any room.

Venetian blinds are great for controlling how much light is filtered into a room as their horizontal slats can be tilted as required. When completely closed they protect furnishings from direct sunlight; tilted at an angle they combine light and privacy; and when the whole blind is pulled right up you get your view on the outside world. Just the thing for contemporary interiors, they provide a structural look in an inexpensive and lively way. Throw a curtain on top and you get a completely different layered look. They are available in a wide variety of materials and colours, so if you fancy a bit of bling then go for something like a gold finish or even neon pink.

Vertical blinds have perpendicular slats so have a similar method of controlling lights to venetian blinds. They are a good choice for shaped windows such as bow and bay windows, as their curved head rails can be bent round to fit snugly. Slat widths vary and colours and styles are numerous, with PVC ones being suitable for steamy areas such as bathrooms.

Roller blinds are perfect for little nooks such as this, adding simple style at reasonable cost. They lighten the mood, block out the neighbours but still let in the light. These blinds have been made to look more whimsical by hanging one of them the opposite way round – subtly making even the easiest of window treatments in vogue.

see also:
texture p125

TOP TIP: Feature lights like this chandelier can become a talking point in themselves.

window treatments
shutters

Classic in feel, shutters give a strong, graphic presence to any room. Unlike curtains they don't crowd a window and, when folded back, allow both the window shape and a lovely view to be revealed. They are hand-crafted to fit so don't come cheap, but like a good piece of furniture they will stand the test of time. Their versatility makes them great for small windows (horizontal slats help broaden narrow widths) and large ones alike. They don't trap dust, making them ideal for allergy sufferers, and require very little maintenance. Couple that with their insulating properties and you have one smart way of adding style.

Louvred shutters are available with both fixed and adjustable horizontal slats of up to about 50mm in depth. They are suitable for most sizes of window as they can be designed in a variety of ways: full length (great for French windows); tier on tier (where the top and bottom halves open separately); or café style (covering just the bottom section of the window). This also allows for greater flexibility in both privacy and light screening. Wooden shutters can be painted or stained to tie in with the colour on your walls, keeping the scheme soothing and unfussy. This type of shutter works especially well in bedrooms and bathrooms – the areas where you need maximum privacy – as the louvres can be angled to allow you to see out, while obscuring visibility from the outside.

An interesting alternative to traditional shutters, panels of Perspex give a contemporary twist to this period window frame. The flat sheets of opaque material allow diffused light into the room, while at the same time providing privacy.

Plantation shutters are similar to louvred shutters but, despite their name, are generally considered more contemporary in style because of their chunkier look. Slats are typically 50mm or more wide and made from wood.

Solid shutters afford maximum privacy and, when closed, act like another wall in your room. Echoing the architecture of the windows, they particularly suit period homes. Unless you are lucky enough to still have the original ones, you can source old shutters from salvage yards and have them cut to fit your windows. But if you fancy something a little more contemporary you can even make your own, giving you ultimate control over the style and material (page 172).

how to...

make Perspex shutters

Out with the nets and in with the Perspex! This super-cool material is an unexpected yet stylish way to give privacy while letting in the light.

shopping list

Perspex
eight hinges
carpenter's pencil
variable-speed drill
  plus bits
nuts and bolts
screws
screwdriver

1 Locate a Perspex supplier near you and ask them to cut a large sheet to the size of the glass and its frame. This should then be cut into four widthways to create the individual, equally sized shutter panels.

2 Lay one piece of Perspex on the floor and place the hinges on each side of the panel at the top and bottom. Make a note of the measurements and with a pencil mark the holes for drilling. Repeat on another panel. These are the two that will be attached to the window frame. Now take the two inner panels and line up with the original to measure and mark the holes on one edge only.

3 Placing an off-cut of wood underneath so as not to mark the floor, drill all the holes for the hinges into each panel (page 181). For delicate materials such as Perspex, it is best to drill a pilot hole first using a small drill bit on a slow speed, to reduce the chance of cracking; then switch to a larger bit.

4 Attach hinges to one side of each of the outer panels using the nuts and bolts, so that the hinges will face into the room. Line up each shutter with the window frame and mark and drill holes for the hinges. Secure the panels to the frame with a screwdriver (page 181).

5 Finally attach the inner panels to the outer panels, with the hinges facing inwards towards the glass. You should now have two pairs of panels hinged together to form your bespoke Perspex shutters. You could stencil or paint onto the Perspex if you want a more decorative effect. Shutters can also be made out of a variety of materials (wood, vinyl, PVC) – you just might need to use heavier hinges as appropriate.

TOP TIP: For really tall windows use thicker Perspex and add additional hinges for support.

practical stuff

tool kit essentials

DIY goes smoothly when you have a good set of tools kept together in an organized way. You only need a minimal selection of tools to be able to tackle most jobs, so don't be tempted to buy that professional-looking 100-piece set – you won't use half of it. Many DIY stores sell great-value starter kits and you can always add other items later if you need something more specialized. It's worth investing in a lidded box to store the tools in and stashing it in an accessible place. That way you'll know instantly where everything is and save yourself a lot of inconvenient trips to and from the garden shed. Big items like pasting tables, stepladders, extension leads and sprayers need storage space of their own, as do all those small bits and bobs like sandpaper, masking tape, cloths and carpenter's pencils. Relegate these to another cupboard to prevent your tool kit from becoming too cluttered.

Tool box – a sturdy, lidded box should be used to store and protect tools; keep in a central location for easy access.

Drill – a variable-speed, cordless drill is the easiest to use; some have adapters that turn them into electric screwdrivers. One with a masonry action and bits is needed for drilling into brick.

Hammer – essential for banging in nails or wallplugs and tapping together adjoining pieces of wood; the claw on the reverse head is also useful for removing nails.

Screwdrivers – a range of screwdrivers with different heads (flat- and cross-head) and in different sizes is invaluable.

Screws, nails and wallplugs – a selection of these in various sizes will be required; check manufacturer's instructions for the right size for the job.

Pliers – can get super-specialized, but combination pliers, suitable for gripping small objects and cutting or bending wire/cable, are the most versatile; long-nose pliers (flat, narrow and strong) are also useful.

Scraper/filling knife – great multi-purpose tool for removing wallpaper and filling holes.

Small cutting tool – available with either fixed or retractable blades; essential for scoring and cutting wallpaper.

Retractable tape measure – key tool for a number of DIY measuring tasks.

Spirit level – the best way of determining a true horizontal; a small, hand-sized one is easier to manipulate. Also indicates verticals.

Plumb line – the easiest method for finding a true vertical line; essential for hanging wallpaper, when a long line is needed.

Face mask – prevents inhalation of dust and paint when sanding and spray painting.

Safety goggles – protection for eyes when sanding or spray painting; also shields from small flying fragments.

tool kit analysis

Store tools in a good, sturdy tool box and keep them close to hand – you never know when you might need them.

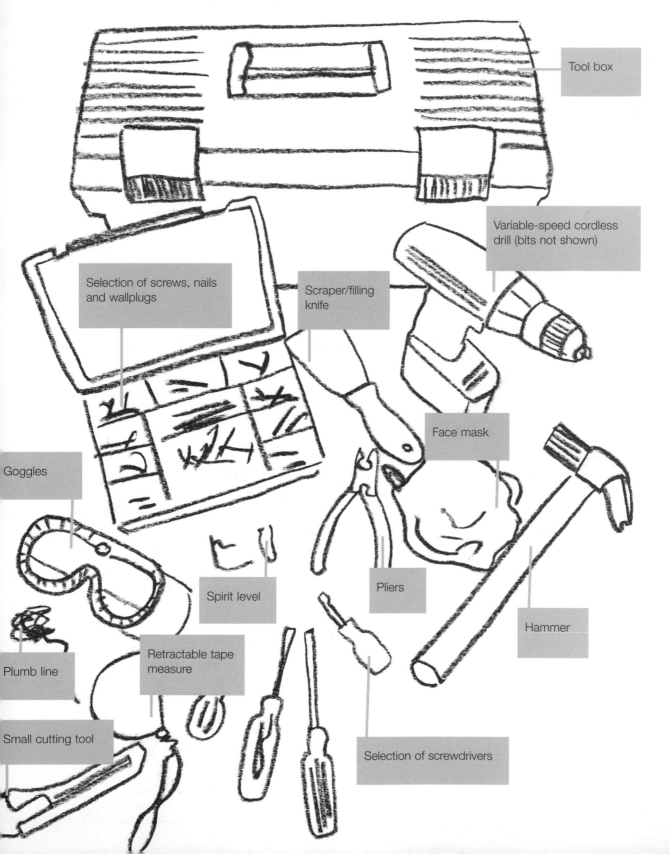

Tool box

Variable-speed cordless drill (bits not shown)

Selection of screws, nails and wallplugs

Scraper/filling knife

Face mask

Goggles

Pliers

Hammer

Spirit level

Plumb line

Retractable tape measure

Small cutting tool

Selection of screwdrivers

tips and techniques

It's been said many times that good preparation takes the bulk of the time in any DIY job, but is essential for making it go smoothly. Well, I'm certainly not one to disagree with that! A thorough clean, good protection of yourself and the surfaces around your home, together with some useful techniques, will take the stress out of decorating and help you achieve the best results.

Keeping clean

Wearing appropriate clothing

DIY can sometimes be a mucky business. Setting aside a set of old clothes especially for decorating will prevent your normal outfits from getting spoiled. You can buy all-in-one overalls from DIY stores but they may only be available in large bloke sizes. A long-sleeved top and comfortable trousers are just as good – just make sure that the sleeves and legs are not too loose and flappy, as they could catch on things and become a safety hazard.

Covering with dust sheets

Dust sheets made from calico or polythene are a must for stopping furniture and floors from being ruined by your decorating project. They are cheap to buy and will save you hours of time cleaning up spills and drips or vacuuming up dust. Secure sheets to the floor with masking tape to prevent them being a trip hazard and, if you are going to reuse them for future projects, make sure any splashes are dry before folding up.

Sealing up rooms to be sanded

Industrial sanding of floorboards is one of the messiest jobs you'll have to do in the home. So to prevent dust from spreading everywhere, first seal the gaps around doors and other openings with masking tape. (Large gaps need to be stuffed with newspaper or rolled dust sheets first.) Try to leave the room as few times as possible to stop dust being dragged underfoot to other areas.

Mopping up spills

Clean up spills as soon as they happen – don't leave the liquid to dry as it will make it more difficult later on. Soapy water will work for most substances, but oil-based paints will need to be cleaned up with white spirit.

Looking after brushes and rollers

Brushes and rollers should be cleaned immediately after use. First, remove excess paint with a paint stirrer or stick (see opposite). If using a water-based product, clean the brush or roller thoroughly in soapy water (the roller sleeve should be removed first). White spirit will remove oil-based paint but don't leave brushes to stand on their bristles in solution for a long period of time as this will cause the brush to lose its shape. Work the white spirit or soapy water through the bristles to ensure all paint is removed. Shake off any excess liquid and dry with a lint-free cloth.

Some simple techniques

Making a mark

Using a special carpenter's pencil to make your mark has several advantages. It has a thicker lead and so is less likely to break. As it is rectangular in shape, you can draw either thin or thick lines by rotating the pencil; and it won't roll away when you put it down.

Masking off

Masking off is an easy way to prevent paint or varnish from going where it shouldn't. It is available in different widths, so choose the appropriate size for the job, but check the instructions to see how long you can leave it in place – the cheaper varieties will only last three or four hours before lifting; more expensive ones can be left up to three days without leaving sticky residue. Tear a strip of tape off the roll and apply to the surface you need to shield, pressing down firmly at the edge to prevent paint from leaking underneath. When the surrounding surfaces are dry, lift the tape away carefully so as not to damage the new decoration. This technique can also be applied to glass when painting window frames.

Hammering in nails

It sounds like a straightforward job, but it's all too easy to bang the wrong nail! First make a mark on the wall with a carpenter's pencil (see opposite) where you want the nail to be. Holding the nail firmly between the fingers towards the sharp end, place it on the wall and gently tap the head. After two or three taps, if the nail has got a hold then remove your hand entirely and hammer more strongly to secure. Leave approximately 10mm proud for hanging objects.

Using a stud finder

A stud finder (variously called a metal or voltage detector) is a useful device designed to detect electricity cables, metal pipes (for water and gas) and wooden wall battens and studs. It's worth investing in this relatively inexpensive piece of kit as it quickly and easily helps you find the best

spot for you to hammer in a nail (see left) or drill a hole (see below). They vary in design – some will make beeping sounds, others have lights that flash – but a sweep over your wall with one of these could prevent you from damaging vital utilities.

Drilling

Before drilling, check for electricity cables, water or gas pipes by using a stud finder (see left). Select the appropriate drill bit for the type of wall you are drilling into (the manufacturer's instructions will tell you). Mark the position on the wall where you want to drill using a carpenter's pencil (see left). Using a hammer and nail, make a small indentation in the wall as this will help prevent the drill bit from slipping. Place the bit at 90 degrees to the wall and gently squeeze the trigger. Apply steady pressure and make sure that you keep the drill as horizontal as you possibly can. Continue drilling until you get to the depth required. (A handy tip is to wrap the drill bit with masking tape at the appropriate depth so that you know when to stop drilling.)

Screwing in by hand

Before using a screw you should always first drill a hole (see above). A hole in a wall needs a wallplug for additional grip. Push it firmly into the cavity and tap with a hammer until it is flush with the wall. Now take the screw, hold it in place with one hand and with the other hand

gently turn the screwdriver to tighten it into the hole. Try to keep the screw and screwdriver horizontal. Fasten until the screw has gone as far in as it can, or if the screw is going to support a mirror or other heavy object (page 36) then leave 10mm proud.

Using a paint kettle

Pouring paint into a paint kettle (a small plastic or metal pot with a handle) has many advantages over painting straight from the tin. It allows you to mix paint from different tins to disguise slight differences in shade. The paint tin can then be sealed up while working to prevent contamination by dust and stray brush hairs . Smaller and lighter than a regular paint tin, a kettle is easier to use up a stepladder. And if you do have a spillage you will have a smaller amount to clear up. Paint kettles are cheap to buy from DIY stores, although any pot with a handle will do the trick.

Stirring paint

A tin of paint will always need a stir before you use it to ensure that all its elements (pigment, oil) are well mixed together. This will help achieve an even coat and finish. Plastic stirrers are available cheaply from DIY stores. Some have holes in the blade for thorough mixing and a comb for scraping paint off brushes, but a simple stick will work just as well – make sure it is long enough to reach the bottom of the paint tin.

tips and techniques

Preparing your surface

Stripping off wallpaper

Removing old wallpaper is messy so first cover furniture and floors with protective sheets (page 180) and have some refuse sacks to hand for the old paper. Soak a sponge in warm water and wet the wallpaper thoroughly to soften the glue. Pick apart a seam and insert a scraper underneath. Lift the paper away from the wall with short, jabbing motions, taking care not to gouge the plaster. Vinyl or thicker wallpaper may prevent water from penetrating, so lightly score the surface first with a small cutting tool to allow moisture to get through. Wet the walls with a home-made solution of one part vinegar to four parts warm water, or a ready-made wallpaper stripping solution, and leave for 30 minutes before scraping off.

Stripping off paint and varnish

Chemical method Ready-made solutions for stripping paint and varnish come in tins, aerosols or spray bottles and most are water washable. If applying from a tin, use an old but good-quality brush to spread the liquid thickly and evenly in one direction over the surface. Leave for the recommended time (normally 20–30 minutes). Remove loose paint with a broad paint scraper, steel wool or old rags – stubborn

spots may require a second coat of remover. Always wear chemical-resistant gloves and a face mask when applying.

Heat method Apply a hot-air gun or blow torch to painted surfaces, keeping it moving to avoid scorching the wood. (You can remove any slight marks by rubbing down with fine sandpaper.) Scrape away the paint as soon as it blisters and peels. Do not use near glass as the heat can cause it to crack. Wear gloves, a face mask and safety goggles.

Sanding Removing paint with sandpaper alone is time-consuming and inefficient; in addition, it is easy to spoil the surface of the wood underneath. Use coarse sandpaper, as the finer grades will clog up quickly. For a finer finish, use one of the preceding methods. Wear a face mask to avoid inhaling dust.

Removing tiles

Removing unwanted wall or floor tiles can be hazardous, so wear safety goggles, a face mask, thick gloves and a long-sleeved top to protect yourself from the sharp edges of broken tiles and flying splinters. Working on one tile at a time, place a large chisel at the back edge and knock with a hammer. Pull the chisel towards you to lever the tile from the wall or floor. For really stubborn tiles, or for removing large floor tiles, use a chisel and a drill fitted with a 'roto

stop' function. A hot-air gun will remove remaining adhesive, but if cement mortar was used you may need to have the wall re-plastered.

Filling a hole or crack

Surfaces such as walls, floors and woodwork should have any chips, cracks or holes filled before you decorate them. Wood filler is ideally suited to filling small to medium holes in wood – choose a colour to match the timber. An all-purpose filler is fine for walls and both this and wood filler are easy to apply, drying quickly ready for painting. A filler such as caulk can be applied with a gun, and so is useful for larger projects. Dislodge any loose material and apply the filler to the crack or hole with a broad filling knife. Wipe away any excess and then smooth the surface over with the blade. Sand when dry for a smooth finish and wash the wall with sugar soap (page 184). For deep holes, apply filler in layers, waiting for each to dry before applying the next.

Priming wood

New wood should be sanded down lightly to smooth the grain and then sugar soaped (page 184). Apply a knotting solution with a brush to knots to stop sap leaking out and spoiling the finished paintwork. Follow with a coat of wood primer.

Priming walls

For painting Primer is specially formulated to seal surfaces,

tips and techniques

making sure paint adheres properly and creating a professional-looking finish. It is a good base coat and, used with an undercoat (see below), may prevent the need to apply two or more coats of your more costly chosen paint. Make sure the wall surface is clean and dry, with any holes and cracks filled (page 183). Apply as you would a topcoat with a roller or paint brush.

For wallpapering All-in-one primer-sealers have all but eliminated the need for traditional wall sizing (the application of a diluted form of wallpaper adhesive). They provide an even, new surface on the wall, making it far easier to slide wallpaper into position and also prevent the wall itself from absorbing too much of the paste. Apply with a pasting brush and leave to dry for the recommended time before hanging wallpaper.

Undercoat

Undercoat is a thick paint which provides good, solid cover for a topcoat. On bare or new surfaces use a primer first (see above). Surfaces that have been painted before need only an undercoat. Remember: an undercoat is always a primer (it provides a smooth, even surface for topcoats); but a primer is not an undercoat – think of it as a base or first coat. An undercoat is particularly useful if the existing shade of paint is darker than the one you intend to apply. Choose one that matches the shade of your topcoat and apply with a roller or paint brush.

Sanding by hand

All wood should be sanded before painting in order to achieve the best finish. Sandpaper is available in different degrees of coarseness, known as grades. The lower the number, the coarser the grade. Most timber should be sanded with medium-grade (120–150) and then finished off with fine (180–220). You also need to lightly sand between coats of paint to provide a 'key' for the next layer. After sanding, surfaces should be sugar soaped and then wiped clean of debris with a lint-free cloth and white spirit (see below).

Cleaning surfaces

Sugar soaping Any surface in the home can become coated with grease and grime. Washing down areas with a grainy liquid called sugar soap ensures that they will be dirt-free, giving the best surface for any further treatments. It is available in powder form for making up yourself or as a ready-made liquid. It is a minor irritant so wear rubber gloves and avoid contact with skin. Work the solution into the wall with a sponge, using a scrubbing motion. Allow to dry, then rinse off with water.

White spirit Wiping down with white spirit also removes grease and should always be done after sanding (see left). Use a lint-free cloth to prevent tiny fibres from being deposited on the surface. White spirit is also a solvent for oil-based paints and should also be used for cleaning paint brushes (page 180) and mopping up spills.

Measuring

Calculating the amount of paint

How much paint you need depends on the size and nature of the surface you are painting. (A smooth, even surface requires less paint than a heavily textured one.) To calculate the number of square metres of your surface multiply the width of the area by the height, remembering to subtract the area of windows, doors and any other fixtures from the calculation. On average, you can reckon on a coverage of ten square metres per litre of paint – for rougher surfaces halve this. Most surfaces will require more than one coat to ensure good coverage.

Calculating the amount of wallpaper

To calculate how many rolls of wallpaper, you first need to measure the perimeter of the room. Divide this figure by the width of the wallpaper to give you X. Divide the length of the roll by the height of the drop you are covering (adding an extra 100mm to the drop for trimming) – this gives you Y. Now divide X by Y to give the number of rolls needed, remembering to round up to the nearest roll. If the wallpaper has a large repeating pattern there will be more wastage, so factor this into your calculations – it is better to overestimate than underestimate. Before unwrapping the rolls check that all the batch numbers are the same, otherwise you run the risk of small differences in colour.

Measuring for curtains

To determine the width and length of curtain you must measure the actual pole or track (not the window), so make sure this is fixed in place first. Measure the total length of the pole/track (excluding finials) and allow a further 25mm for the curtains to overlap in the centre when closed. Decide on the drop you require (typically curtains are hung to the floor, to the sill or just below) and measure the distance from the top of the pole/track to the required length. Remember that where the curtain actually sits on the pole will vary according to your choice of heading (page 166). Curtain suppliers and makers will be able to advise you on how much material you need to cover this area – the rule of thumb is two and a half times, but it will also depend on the style of heading and the thickness of the material.

Measuring for blinds

First decide whether you want the blind to sit inside or outside the window recess (if there is one). The recess needs to be at least 75mm

deep to take the mechanism. Note the width and length of the recess in several places to allow for irregularities. If the window doesn't have a recess, or you want to block out the light, the blind needs to be fixed above the window frame. Measure the width of this, allowing an additional 50mm either side to adequately cover the frame. Now take a note of the length, adding an extra 40mm to allow for the mechanism. Once again, measure in different places to avoid costly mistakes.

Keeping safe

Electricity, gas and water

Always switch the electricity supply off when working with lighting or power sockets. You don't need to turn off all the mains, just the power to that particular area of the home. Water and electricity are a potentially lethal mix so even if you're only washing walls, turn off electrics if there are any sockets mounted there. For the same reason avoid using electric tools such as a drill or paint sprayer in damp conditions. Make sure you know where the stopcock is and that you can easily turn it off in the event of a burst water pipe or flood, and never touch a gas appliance except to clean it. If in doubt always consult a qualified professional (page 187).

Using a stepladder

A stepladder is the safest way of reaching heights – never use a

chair as they are not designed to distribute weight and can easily tip or break. Always follow the manufacturer's instructions to ensure that the stepladder is correctly assembled. Rest the legs on a solid surface at the bottom and check that it is stable before mounting. Wear sensible shoes (no bare feet or high heels, girls) and don't be tempted to overreach – always get down and move the stepladder to the required position.

Ensuring good ventilation

Always make sure that the room is properly ventilated when working with oil-based paint and varnish to avoid inhaling strong fumes. Open doors and windows to allow a good supply of fresh air to flow through and to enable fumes to escape. Wear a face mask to increase protection.

Looking after yourself

Following the basic precautions listed above should help protect you from most hazards. In addition, you should tie long hair back to prevent it getting trapped in things and wear flat, covered shoes (not sandals) to protect the soles and tops of your feet. Keep a basic first-aid kit to hand for minor injuries and have a battery-operated torch to hand in case of power failure. Always use the right tools for the job – don't improvise. Most important, though, is to take regular breaks so that you don't lose concentration or make mistakes through tiredness.

useful contacts

DIY stores

B&Q
Tel: 0845 609 6688
www.diy.com

Focus
Tel: 0800 436436
www.focusdiy.co.uk

Homebase
Tel: 0845 077 8888
www.homebase.co.uk

Travis Perkins
Tel: 01604 752424
www.travisperkins.co.uk

Wickes
Tel: 0845 279 9898
www.wickes.co.uk

Architectural salvage yards

Drew Pritchard
Llanrwst Road, Glan Conwy,
Conwy, Wales LL28 5TH
Tel: 01492 580890
www.drewpritchard.co.uk

Drummonds
The Kirkpatrick Buildings,
25 London Road, Hindhead,
Surrey GU26 6AB
Tel: 01428 609444
www.drummonds-arch.co.uk

also at 78 Royal Hospital Road,
London SW3 4HN
Tel: 020 7376 4499

Holyrood Architectural Salvage
Holyrood Business Park,
146 Duddingston Road, West
Edinburgh, Scotland EH16 4AP
Tel: 0131 661 9305
www.holyroodarchitecturalsalvage.com

Lassco
30 Wandsworth Road, Vauxhall,
London SW8 2LG
Tel: 020 7394 2100
www.lassco.co.uk

also at London Road, Milton
Common, Oxfordshire OX9 2JN
Tel: 01844 277188

Robert Mills
Narroways Road, Eastville,
Bristol BS2 9XB
Tel: 01179 556542
www.rmills.co.uk

Salvo
www.salvo.co.uk (website only)

Trainspotters
Unit 1, The Warehouse,
Libby Drive, Stroud,
Gloucestershire GL5 1RN
Tel: 01453 756677
www.trainspotters.uk.com

Westland London
St Michael's Church, Leonard
Street, London EC2A 4QX
Tel: 020 7739 8094
www.westlandlondon.com

Wilson's Yard
123 Killsborough Road, Dromore,
County Down, Northern Ireland
BT25 1QW
Tel: 028 9269 2304
www.wilsonsyard.com

Stockists

Atelier Abigail Ahern
(homeware)
137 Upper Street, Islington,
London N1 1QP
Tel: 020 7354 8181
www.atelierabigailahern.com

Designers Guild
(homeware, paint, wallpaper)
277 Kings Road,
London SW3 5EN
Tel: 020 7351 5775
www.designersguild.com

Farrow & Ball
(paint)
Uddens Estate, Wimborne,
Dorset BH21 7NL
Tel: 01202 876141
www.farrow-ball.com

Gilbert Curry Industrial Plastics
(Perspex)
16 Bayton Road, Bayton Industrial
Estate, Coventry, West Midlands
CV7 9EJ
Tel: 02476 588388
www.gcip.co.uk

Ikea
(flat-pack furniture)
Various branches nationwide.
Tel: 0845 358 3363 (online shop)
www.ikea.com

Jonathan Trotter
(door handles)
Email only:
trotterjonathan@hotmail.com
jonathantrotter.blogspot.com

Lisa Bengtsson
(wallpaper)
Studio Lisa Bengtsson, Atlasgatan
14, 113 20 Stockholm, Sweden
Tel: 00 46 70 57 99 345
www.lisabengtsson.se

Squint
(upholstery, lighting, accessories)
178 Shoreditch High Street,
London E1 6HU
Tel: 020 7739 9275
www.squintlimited.com

Timorous Beasties
(wallpaper)
384 Great Western Road,
Glasgow, Scotland G4 9HT
Tel: 0141 337 2622

also at 46 Amwell Street,
London EC1R 1XS
Tel: 020 7833 5010
www.timorousbeasties.com

Wild At Heart
(flowers, homeware)
54 Pimlico Road,
London SW1W 8LP
Tel: 020 7229 1174
www.wildatheart.com

Zoffany
(paint & wallpaper)
Chalfont House,
Oxford Road, Denham,
Buckinghamshire UB9 4DX
Tel: 0844 543 4600
www.zoffany.uk.com

Good sources of junk items

Ardingly Fair
East of England Showground,
Ardingly, West Sussex RH17 6TL
www.dmgantiquefairs.com

Clignancourt flea market
Paris
www.parispuces.com/FR

Newark Fair
Newark & Nottinghamshire
Showground, Winthorpe, Newark,
Nottinghamshire NG24 2NY
www.dmgantiquefairs.com

Portobello Road
London W11
www.portobelloroad.co.uk

Websites for free stuff

Freecycle
www.freecycle.org

Gumtree
www.gumtree.com

Design blogs

www.apartmenttherapy.com
www.coolhunting.com
www.decor8blog.com
www.designersblock.blogspot.com
www.designspongeonline.com
www.designspotter.com
www.mocoloco.com
www.peakofchic.com
www.sfgirlbybay.com
www.stylebeat.blogspot.com

Trade organisations

Will help you find an approved
contractor.

Electricity
NICEIC
Tel: 0870 013 0382
www.niceic.org.uk

Gas
CORGI
Tel: 0800 915 0485
www.trustcorgi.com

Water
The Association of Plumbing and
Heating Contractors (APHC)
Tel: 02476 470626
www.competentpersonscheme.
co.uk

index

index

*acknowledgements

Author's acknowledgements

The hugest thank you to Anne Furniss and Helen Lewis at Quadrille for giving me this fabulous opportunity and for being so brilliant and supportive. Thanks also to Pauline Savage for editing my ramblings so forensically and patiently. I would also like to thank Graham Atkins-Hughes, whose photography, as always, is beyond exquisite.

This book would not have come together without all the wonderful people who opened their doors to allow us to photograph their beautiful homes:

Nikki Tibbles, florist and founder of Wild at Heart (www.wildatheart.com)

Interior designer Michael Bargo at Michael Bargo Inc (email: ny73@mac.com)

Designer Lorraine Kirke and her fabulous store (www.geminola.com)

Rita Konig, style writer, interior decorator and editor at large for Domino magazine (www.dominomag.com)

Designer Gemma Ahern and wallpaper designer Russell Lewis (www.underthebridge.org)

Designer Lisa Whatmough (www.squintlimited.com)

On a personal note, thank you to Gemma and Graham for absolutely everything; to my wonderful parents for being a constant inspiration; and to Gillian and Alan for their unrelenting support and commitment.

Publisher's acknowledgements

The publishers would like to thank John Peacock and Wendy Kyte of Lewisham College for technical advice; also Gary at Able Skills.

The author and publisher take no responsibility for any injury or loss arising from the procedures or materials described in this book. Materials, tools, skills and work areas vary greatly and are the responsibility of the reader. Follow the manufacturer's instructions and take the appropriate safety precautions.

Editorial director
Anne Furniss
Art director
Helen Lewis
Project editor
Pauline Savage
Designer
Katherine Case
Photography
Graham Atkins-Hughes
Production
Marina Asenjo, Vincent Smith

First published in 2009 by Quadrille Publishing Limited Alhambra House 27-31 Charing Cross Road London WC2H 0LS

Reprinted in 2009, 2010 (twice)
10 9 8 7 6 5 4

Text © 2009 Abigail Ahern Design and layout © 2009 Quadrille Publishing Limited Photography © 2009 Graham Atkins-Hughes

The author's designs may be followed for personal use only and not for commercial purposes.

A catalogue record for this book is available from the British Library.

ISBN: 9781844007301

Printed and bound in China